FACING THE
AGE WAVE

The Hoover Institution
gratefully acknowledges generous support from

TAD TAUBE
TAUBE FAMILY FOUNDATION
KORET FOUNDATION

Founders of the Program on
American Institutions and Economic Performance

and Cornerstone gifts from

JOANNE AND JOHAN BLOKKER
SARAH SCAIFE FOUNDATION

FACING THE AGE WAVE

Edited by
DAVID A. WISE

Hoover Institution Press
Stanford University
Stanford, California

Hoover Institution Press Publication No. 440

Copyright © 1997 by the Board of Trustees of the
    Leland Stanford Junior University

Cover photo credit: Stanford University, Visual Arts Services, Steve Gladfelter

First printing, 1997
03 02 01 00 99 98 97   9 8 7 6 5 4 3 2 1

Manufactured in the United States of America

The paper used in this publication meets the minimum requirements
of American National Standard for Information Sciences—Permanence
of Paper for Printed Library Materials, ANSI Z39.48–1984. ∞

Library of Congress Cataloging-in-Publication Data
Facing the age wave / edited by David A. Wise.
        p.   cm. — (Hoover Institution Press publication ; no. 440)
    Includes bibliographical references and index.
    ISBN 0-8179-9482-3 (alk. paper)
    1. Aged—Government policy—United States.   2. Aged—United
States—Economic conditions.   3. Aged—Medical care—United States.
4. Retirement income—United States.   5. United States—Economic
policy.   6. United States—Social policy.   I. Wise, David A.
II. Series: Hoover Institution Press publication : 440.
HQ1064.U5F23   1997
362.6'0973—dc21   97-14133
                                                        CIP

Contents

David A. Wise

Introduction

The aging of the American population magnifies many issues of public concern. The U.S. Social Security system will be broke by 2029, according to government projections; Medicare will begin to run enormous deficits in the next few years. The financial problems faced by these programs are due in part to provisions in those programs that were apparently adopted without adequately understanding their financial implications. But an aging population makes these problems loom larger and, indeed, is on a collision course with trends in individual behavior as well. Douglas Bernheim, David Cutler, John Shoven, and I discuss three critical issues that must be addressed if government policy and individual behavior are to adapt gracefully to the coming age wave. As the population ages, a larger and larger fraction of retired Americans will have to be supported by their previous savings or by the declining fraction of the working population. The demographic trends that have created this problem are exacerbated by older Americans retiring at increasingly younger ages. The fact that a large fraction of Americans saves little increases the pressure on an already financially pressed Social Security system. Yet recent tax legislation may be doing as much to discourage as to encourage personal saving, perhaps contributing to the dearth of saving. Health care costs are increasing at the same time that the number of older heavy users of health care is increasing.

My chapter directs attention to the declining labor force participation of older Americans and the role Social Security and employer-provided pension plans play in encouraging early retirement. Douglas Bernheim looks at the inadequacy of personal retirement saving and discusses what might be done to encourage such saving. John Shoven and I point to the taxing of pensions as an illustration of tax policy run awry that may substantially limit retirement saving, the most important form of saving in America. David Cutler helps us understand the nature of the looming health care problem and proposes principles that might be followed in addressing the problem.

The confluence of early retirement with a rapidly aging population is unlikely to be sustainable and will have to be addressed if the federal budget is to be balanced. In chapter 1, "More Older People Living Longer, Working Less," I review these trends and explore how Social Security and employer-provided pension plans in particular have provided substantial incentive to leave the labor force early.

In effect, work after a given age is taxed, often as young as fifty-five, under employer-provided plans. The quantitative effect of this inducement is illustrated by estimating the effects of changes in pension plan and Social Security provisions on the retirement decisions of employees in a large firm who are covered by a typical defined benefit pension plan. Scheduled Social Security changes have little effect on the retirement decisions of employees with such a plan. But if the pension plan provisions are changed to correspond to the Social Security changes, the predicted effect is large. Although apparently not contemplated by current legislation, it is also clear that an increase in the Social Security early retirement age would substantially affect the early retirement rates of the large number of employees not covered by a pension plan.

The major reason for the existence of pension plans is to allow workers to retire with a secure source of income. Thus it should be

expected, and welcomed, that increased pension coverage allows workers to retire earlier. The issue, however, is not that the accumulation of
pension benefits allows retirement but rather that the typical accumulation pattern penalizes the continued labor force participation of elderly workers. Even if the total entitlement is relatively small, the accrual pattern may mean a large bonus for remaining in the firm until
a given age and then a large loss for staying. At certain ages, the decision to continue working likely means that a large fraction of wage
earnings is offset through a loss in the value of future pension benefits.
After sixty-five, this is also the case with Social Security benefits. If there
is a problem with the current structure of pensions, it is that it constrains the choice of older workers to continue in the labor force.
Whether this is the optimal plan structure in light of current demographic trends is open to question.

What might be done? I suggest movement in four directions: The
first is to increase the Social Security retirement age. An increase in
the retirement age from sixty-five to sixty-seven is planned but too far
off. One natural path is to increase the Social Security retirement age
by one month a year, which over the past several decades has been the
approximate annual increase in life expectancy at sixty-five. The early
retirement age, now sixty-two, should also be increased.

The second, on the employer side, is to move from defined benefit
to defined contribution plans (where the benefit is determined by how
much is contributed to the pension fund). Switching to defined contribution plans has two major advantages: There would be no artificial
incentives created by implicit subsidies and taxes on labor force participation, such as those inherent in the typical defined benefit plan. In
addition, pension entitlements could be transferred from one job to
another with the employee. Changing jobs would thus not engender
losses in pension entitlement, and labor mobility would not be artificially discouraged. To some extent, the ongoing expansion of 401(k)
plans in particular and traditional employer-provided defined contribution plans is moving in this direction.

The third direction is gradual, rather than abrupt, withdrawal from the labor force. The vast majority of workers now go from full-time work to retirement overnight. Current institutional arrangements make gradually withdrawing from the labor force extremely difficult. The problem of course is not simply that firms are reluctant to do it but employees are also not used to such arrangements.

The fourth direction is encouraging personal saving for retirement. I believe that this is best done through continued expansion and promotion of 401(k) plans and resurrection of the individual retirement account (IRA) program, which largely disappeared after the Tax Reform Act of 1986.

In chapter 2, "The Adequacy of Personal Retirement Saving: Issues and Options," Douglas Bernheim discusses the problems of paying for retirement in the twenty-first century and policy options, including ways to encourage greater personal saving. He emphasizes that, over the next few decades, new retirees will likely become increasingly reliant on voluntary personal saving. He foresees that the cost of retirement will rise and that retirees will find it increasingly difficult to meet these costs without personal saving. In particular he foresees that the fraction of preretirement income replaced by Social Security will decline over the next few decades and explains why conventional employer-provided pension plans and private transfers from older to younger generations are unlikely to fill the gap. If the preretirement standard of living is to be maintained, which Bernheim emphasizes is the typical goal and *expectation* of younger generations looking ahead to retirement, personal saving is not nearly enough to achieve this goal.

He finds that baby boomers in particular are saving at only 33 to 38 percent of the rate required to meet their expectations under the present Social Security benefits. Using more-realistic assumptions about the future of Social Security, he finds that baby boomers are saving at only 22 percent of the rate required to cover their expected retirement costs. In a worst-case scenario, without Social Security, baby boomers are saving only 12 percent of what they need to meet their goals.

Bernheim goes on to suggest possible ways to increase personal saving. First, based on his evaluation of the evidence, he concludes that eligibility for a 401(k) plan significantly stimulates personal saving as a result of several factors: The contribution limit is high relative to the typical saving of most individuals, and employers often match employee contributions. Emphasizing that 401(k) saving plans can capitalize on the "psychology of saving," he notes that contributions are by payroll deduction and thus may provide a form of self-discipline. Once part of the plan, individuals do not have to decide to make discretionary deposits. (I have also focused on this aspect of 401(k) plans as providing a means of self-control, taking advantage of the out-of-sight, out-of-mind principle.) Bernheim also points out that the higher contribution limits may validate higher saving rates; presumably, if the limits are high, someone must think that saving this much is appropriate. Finally, he notes that the workplace environment allows employee discussions that may encourage saving and that the growth of 401(k)s has promoted retirement saving education in the workplace.

He emphasizes more generally the power of promotion and education programs to encourage personal saving. In addition to the explosion of education in the workplace, he points to the Labor Department's national pension education program, which draws the attention of American workers to the importance of taking responsibility for their retirement security. Pointing to the saving promotion campaigns launched by the Japanese government after World War II, he concludes that the public sector could play an important role in promoting saving awareness and establishing saving as a highly visible national priority.

Tax legislation over the past fifteen years may have done just the opposite, however. In chapter 3, "Keeping Savers from Saving," John Shoven and I describe the legislation that explains this allegory: John

David A. Wise

Saver died at age seventy leaving an estate worth $1.9 million dollars; his wife had died two years earlier. He had saved conscientiously throughout his lifetime, hoping to have a long and comfortable retirement and believing that, were he to die prematurely, his children would benefit from his saving. Most of his saving was through a defined contribution pension plan to which he and his employer had contributed throughout his career. The contributions, which were placed each month in a stock fund, had accumulated to $1.2 million by the time of his death. Not knowing exactly what his firm plan would be worth, he had also saved through a personal individual retirement account in which he had accumulated $100,000. He had a house and other assets worth $600,000. He was confident that, by consuming a bit less and saving a bit more while he was working, his children would be much better off than the children of his friend Jimmy Spender, who had saved little. In 1982, John Saver would have been right. At that time his children would have been left with $60,000 of the last $100,000 that John had saved. But in 1996 he was wrong. His children were left with only $15,000 of this $100,000. Although John didn't know it—because he had worked until seventy and had not thought to check for hidden legislation—had he started to withdraw saving from his retirement plans at age seventy, he would have paid a marginal tax rate of 61.5 percent on his retirement income.

What happened was that during this period the introduction of IRA and 401(k) saving plans provided a large inducement to save, and a large body of evidence shows that contributions to these plans have worked to increase personal saving. Indeed, saving through those plans now far exceeds saving through traditional employer-provided defined benefit and defined contribution pension plans. At the same time, however, and virtually hidden from the public eye, congressional legislators imposed harsh penalties on persons who unwittingly chose to save too much in retirement accounts. Whereas in 1982 pension assets were not subject to any estate taxes, by 1985 they were fully taxed as part of the estate. In addition, the excess distribution and excess accumulation taxes, the so-called success taxes, had been slipped into the 1986 tax legislation. Possibly 80 percent of total personal saving is by way of employer or personal pension plans. Virtually all thoughtful observers believe that Americans save too little and that the low saving rate will limit future economic growth nationwide and, at a personal level, will endanger the economic well-being of future elderly Americans. Why then, we ask, are the most consistent savers penalized?

We consider the evolution of the legislation that created virtually confiscatory tax rates on pension assets. Although we focus on the taxation of only one type of saving—albeit the singlemost important saving vehicle in the United States—we hope that the analysis and discussion will direct attention to laws that seem to us hard to justify. Thinking of this chapter as a case study of tax legislation gone awry, we find that the marginal tax rate on large distributions is likely to be as high as 61.5 percent and that the confiscatory marginal tax rates on large pension assets passing through an estate can be as high as 92 to 97 percent and sometimes even higher. Considering who might be affected by these tax rates now and who may be affected in the future, we conclude that these taxes are not limited to the wealthy. Indeed, consistent savers with modest earnings who invest prudently may also be faced with these penalty taxes. Rather than taxes on the rich, these are widespread penalties on lifetime savers. Although most families who are on the eve of retirement have saved little, as personal saving plans spread, a large proportion of lifetime savers could face excess distribution tax rates on retirement income withdrawn from these accounts. Many of these families would see their saving virtually confiscated if they died with substantial assets in retirement accounts. Many lifetime savers will find that the prospect of these taxes completely offsets the incentive to save for retirement in a pension plan. Knowing that most of the funds will be confiscated if pension assets remain at death provides an enormous incentive to limit pension saving. Furthermore, these taxes provide a large incentive to withdraw saving from pension funds before it is needed. All the above work to limit the saving of those who would otherwise save the most.

We explore the forces that have led to such legislation and conclude that, if economic growth is to be quickened and if the well-being of future elderly is to be enhanced, the relative power of these forces will have to change. America can only be hurt by keeping savers from saving.

Americans' leaving the labor force at younger and younger ages magnifies the problem of providing support for those who are retired. Ironically, the very government and employer-provided pension plans that were intended to support retirement have provided the incentives for early retirement, which in turn increases the resources necessary to support older Americans. At the same time the personal saving of future retirees is not nearly large enough to provide the standard of living in retirement that these future retirees want and expect. Even if current generations are saving the same as past generations, they are working less and thus their retirement needs are greater. Yet a good part of government legislation works to reduce rather than increase saving. In the face of an aging population, early retirement and minimal saving are two critical issues. A third issue that interacts with the first two to make more urgent the need for change is the cost of medical care. In chapter 4, "Medical Care Reform for an Aging Society," David Cutler helps us understand the nature of the looming health care problem and proposes principles that might be followed in attempting to address the problem.

Nearly 14 percent of national income in the United States is spent on medical care, perhaps twice as much as in most other developed countries. Projections suggest spending of more than 25 percent of gross domestic product by 2030. Part of the projected increase comes from population aging; the cost for persons eighty-five and older is approximately twelve times as high as the average cost for persons nineteen to sixty-four. But the cost is rising for all ages. Cutler emphasizes that this increase is likely due in large part to the use of technologically advanced procedures. For example, the increase in the cost of treating heart attack patients is due almost entirely to the prevalence of intensive treatment methods. What do we get from such high-cost treatments? Cutler speculates that over the past thirty years high-technology treatments have probably increased the health of the typical American. But he also speculates that, "at the margin," any further spread of high-technology treatments is likely to be low. He argues that current insurance policies—with patients paying little for care when it is received and doctors paid more for additional care—create incentives for the development of high-technology, high-cost medical procedures and minimize the value of cost-saving technologies. A new technology that offers marginal improvements in health but has high cost, for example, will be demanded widely if patients themselves pay little for its use. At the same time, a new technology that offers slightly worse care but at substantially lower cost will not be sought out if patients do not perceive the cost saving. Cutler suggests that the "dynamic moral hazard" may explain why technology in medicine is almost uniformly associated with cost increases.

Cutler goes on to consider options for reform. He first emphasizes that policies that simply shift the cost from the public sector to the private sector do not help; the ultimate cost to the patient is not reduced. Cost shifting does not make the market for medical care more efficient. He also argues that legislated reductions in payments to providers cannot save medical care costs. This, he points out, rules out the source of most of the savings that the public sector (as well as the private sector) has realized in recent years. "This is unfortunate," he concludes. What can help?

Cutler proposes that people be given the financial incentives to make more appropriate choices about their medical care through the insurance system. If people share in the cost of more generous insurance (through higher premiums) and receive the benefits of less generous insurance (through lower premiums), insurance providers will

David A. Wise

have the incentives to design better insurance policies—ones that provide only care that is worth more to the patient than its cost. Such "choice-based" insurance systems allow patients to choose the services they want. Implementing such systems poses important obstacles, however, and Cutler discusses these as well. The most important is self-selection, with those who plan to spend a lot, or those who expect to be ill, selecting the more generous and expensive plans. Also needed is a mechanism to adjust plan premiums for the health mix (or the health expenditure propensity) of persons who choose a particular insurance plan. Cutler concludes that a choice-based system holds the promise of reducing medical care costs in the long run.

1   *David A. Wise*

More Older People Living Longer, Working Less

The U.S. population is aging rapidly, and individuals are living longer. Yet older Americans are leaving the labor force at younger and younger ages. The prospect is that a shrinking proportion of labor force participants will be supporting a growing fraction of retired persons. These trends are unlikely to be sustainable and will have to be addressed if the federal budget is to be brought into balance. I review these trends and then explore the important role that Social Security and employer-provided pension plans have played in inducing early retirement.

The rapid changes in the age of the population are dramatically shown by the Bureau of the Census graphs in figure 1. In 1950, the population was described by the pyramid shape, with a large supporting base of young men and women supporting a much smaller proportion of older persons. Projections for the year 2030, however, present a much different picture: the pyramid is now almost a square, with the weight of the older population almost equal to the weight of the younger population.

I am grateful to the National Institute on Aging and the Hoover Institution for financial support. Components of this paper have been abstracted from Wise (1997).

David A. Wise

Not only is there an ongoing increase in the proportion of the older population, but life expectancy at older ages is increasing as well. Between 1960 and 1990, life expectancy of men at age fifty-five increased by more than 16 percent and life expectancy at age sixty-five increased about 18 percent (see figure 2). The life expectancy of women at age fifty-five increased almost 15 percent and at age sixty-five increased about 20 percent over this period.

Yet over approximately the same period, the labor force participation of men declined enormously. The decline between 1960 and 1993 is shown in figure 3. The proportion of men aged sixty-five and over in the labor force declined 52 percent over this period, and the decline for men aged sixty to sixty-four was 35 percent. Even at younger ages the decline was noticeable, with a 15 percent drop for men aged fifty-five to fifty-nine and about a 7 percent drop for men aged fifty to fifty-four.

In the next section, I confirm that increased saving is not the explanation for early retirement. In the second section, the effects of Social Security and employer-provided pension plans on retirement are illustrated and the potential effects of health status and health insurance are raised. How changes in employer-provided pension plan provisions, and in Social Security provisions, might affect retirement decisions is discussed in the third section. In the fourth section, I summarize the evidence and suggest policy directions that I believe would work to address the inevitable collision between the accelerating aging of the population and the rapid departure of the elderly from the labor force in the face of little personal saving for retirement.

Wealth at Retirement

The low U.S. national saving rate has been a continuing source of concern because it is likely to limit future economic growth. Low personal saving also reduces the individual well-being of older Americans. Here I want to make clear that the presence of personal saving is not an explanation for earlier retirement and to set out the sources of retirement support. Douglas Bernheim (in this volume) presents a more general discussion of saving in the United States.

Social Security benefits provide the vast majority of the income of a large fraction of retired Americans, and the present value of expected future benefits is the major component of the wealth of most elderly families. In 1991, the median Social Security wealth of families with heads aged sixty-five to sixty-nine was about $100,000 (see figure 4a). Median employer-provided pension wealth (including government and military pensions) was only $16,017. Pension wealth is distributed much more unevenly than Social Security wealth—44 percent of families with heads aged sixty-five to sixty-nine have no pension income. The median level of housing equity was $50,000, but housing equity is typically not used to support consumption of the elderly, at least not until quite advanced ages.[1] The median level of other nonliquid assets, such as cars and business equity, was only $5,992. Personal saving through conventional channels represents a very small proportion of the assets of most older families; the median level of personal financial assets, excluding individual retirement account (IRA) and 401(k) assets, was only $7,428.[2] Thus most families, if they spend the income provided by Social Security and employer pension annuities, have almost no liquid assets accessible to meet unexpected expenditures. More than half of families had neither IRA nor 401(k) accounts; thus their median wealth in personal retirement assets was zero.

Although the median is the best single measure of the assets of the typical family, the components of wealth other than Social Security are highly skewed, making the means much larger than the medians.

---

1. See Venti and Wise (1989, 1990, 1991), Feinstein and McFadden (1989), and Sheiner and Weil (1992).

2. The value for 1991 may be an anomaly. Medians in earlier years were about $9,000, and mean values increased from about $34,365 in 1984 to $42,018 in 1991.

Figure 1   U.S. Population, by Age and Sex: 1950, 1989, and 2030

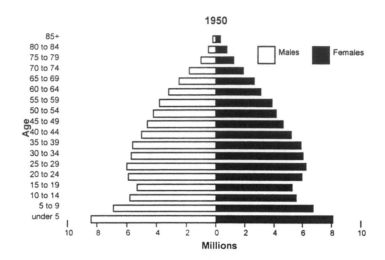

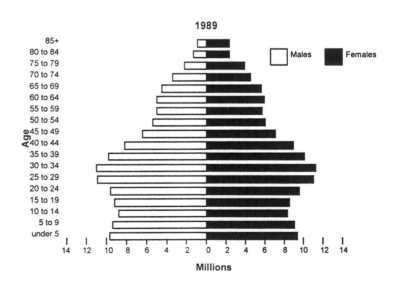

SOURCES: U.S. Bureau of the Census (1965, 1969, and 1990)

Figure 1   (*continued*)

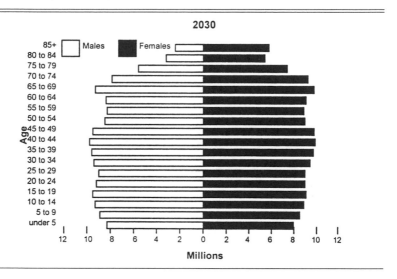

Figure 2.   Life Expectancy (Percent increase, 1960 to 1990)

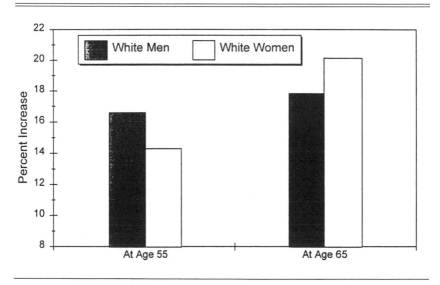

SOURCE: *Vital Statistics of the U.S.*

David A. Wise

Figure 3   Male Labor Force Participation
            (Percent decline, 1960 to 1993)

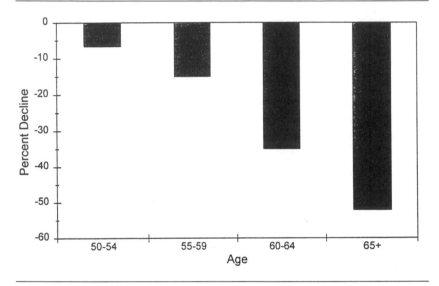

SOURCE: Bureau of Labor Statistics, *Employment and Earnings*

The mean level of other personal financial assets in 1991 was $42,018, more than five times the median. But even mean personal financial assets are a small fraction of combined Social Security and employer-provided pension assets, as indicated in figure 4b. The means reveal the increasing importance of IRA and 401(k) assets as a fraction of total personal financial assets. For families with heads aged sixty-five to sixty-nine, personal retirement assets were only 6.6 percent of total personal financial assets in 1984; by 1991, they represented 20.6 percent. Personal retirement assets increased more than fourfold between 1984 and 1991, much more than any other component of wealth.

   The potential of promised Social Security benefits to reduce personal saving—even though the unfunded Social Security system does not contribute to national saving—has been the subject of economic discussion for many years, with no consensus on the magnitude of the effect. Most studies find little trade-off between employer-provided

Figure 4   Median and Mean Assets by Category
             (Families aged 65 to 69 in 1991)

a. Median Assets

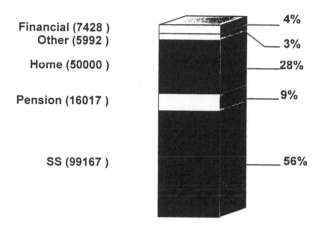

Financial (7428)   4%
Other (5992)   3%

Home (50000)   28%

Pension (16017)   9%

SS (99167)   56%

b. Mean Assets

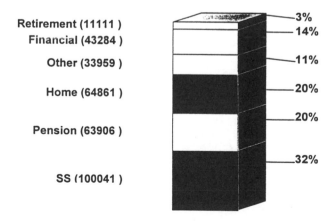

Retirement (11111)   3%
Financial (43284)   14%

Other (33959)   11%

Home (64861)   20%

Pension (63906)   20%

SS (100041)   32%

NOTE: The figure shows percents only to convey the relative amounts of each asset; in fact medians
are not additive, so that the sum of the individual medians is not equal to the median of the sum.
SOURCE: Author's tabulation from the Survey of Income and Program Participation

David A. Wise

pension wealth and personal financial assets, suggesting that employer pensions do indeed increase saving. Although the *saving* effect of these programs may be unclear, there is essentially no dispute that pensions and Social Security have reduced labor force participation and thus the *earnings* of older Americans, as discussed in the next section.

Pension Plans, Social Security, and Other Inducements to Retire

BACKGROUND: TRENDS IN LABOR FORCE PARTICIPATION RATES

Early departures from the labor force may have been made possible by and attributed to the introduction of Social Security and firm pension plans. These programs can lead to younger retirement for two reasons. First, they provide a means of support during retirement, so that people can afford to retire. (Of course, the major reason for retirement programs is to do just this.) Second, and more worrisome, the benefit structure of these programs includes financial incentives that encourage retirement and penalize work. Neither Social Security nor firm pension plans have been neutral with respect to the age individuals decide to retire. Rather, both their provisions encourage early retirement and penalize continuing participation in the labor force.

According to a recent study, the labor force participation rates of men over sixty were essentially constant between 1870 and 1930 and then declined continuously thereafter.[3] The data on labor force participation, based on the decennial censuses, can be used to construct labor force participation rates by age group for men and women at ten-year intervals, beginning in 1940.[4] The rates for men fell in each age

---

3. See Ransom and Sutch (1988).
4. See Sandefur and Tuma (1987).

group. For example, 61.4 percent of men aged fifty-five and over were in the labor force in 1940; by 1970 the proportion had fallen to 52.7 percent; and by 1990 only 39.4 percent of men in this age group were in the labor force. The participation rates of women aged fifty-five and over increased until 1970. Since 1970, however, even the participation rates for older women have fallen.

The decrease in labor force participation rates after 1930 roughly corresponds to the implementation of the Social Security program and federal tax incentives for private pension plans. Social Security was introduced under the Social Security Act of 1935. Company pensions were spurred by the Revenue Act of 1942, which granted tax incentives to firms to establish pension plans. The correlation between the introduction of these retirement policies and the change in labor force participation at older ages suggests that the policies may have induced younger retirement. Many researchers have pointed to the Social Security system's high benefit levels and work disincentives as a major contributor to the continuing trend toward early retirement, and a great deal of research has focused on the effect of Social Security on labor force participation. More recent research has identified similar but more pronounced work disincentives in most private pension plans.[5]

Roughly three-quarters of all persons participating in private pension plans are enrolled in defined benefit plans where benefits are determined according to a specified formula. The remainder are enrolled in plans where benefits are directly related to contributions made on behalf of the employee and to the performance of the plan's investment portfolio. Because a large fraction of workers are covered by defined benefit plans and because they are likely to have the greatest effects on labor market behavior, the discussion here emphasizes the incentive effects of this type of plan.

---

5. See Kotlikoff and Wise (1987, 1988, 1989a, 1989b), Lumsdaine, Stock, and Wise (1990, 1991, 1992, 1994a, 1994b, 1995), and Stock and Wise (1990a, 1990b).

David A. Wise

Figure 5   Retirement with Defined Benefit Plan (Fortune 500 firm)

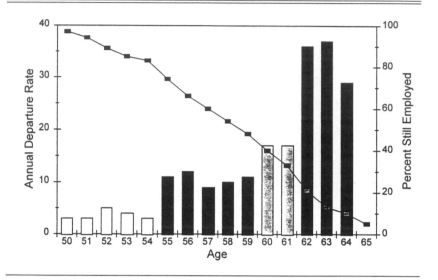

The effects of Social Security and pension incentives (independent of the retirement wealth they represent) on retirement decisions may be illustrated by considering the relationship between pension plan/ Social Security provisions and retirement in a firm. Kotlikoff and Wise (1989a), in a study of a large Fortune 500 firm, show a strong relationship between the economic incentives in the retirement policies and departure rates from the firm. The proportion of the firm's employees who leave at each age (beginning with age fifty) are shown in figure 5. The annual departure rate is the proportion of those employed at the beginning of the year that retires—more strictly speaking, leaves the firm—during that same year. About 3 percent of the employees between ages fifty and fifty-four leave each year. The departure rate jumps to about 11 percent at age fifty-five. There is another jump at age sixty and again at ages sixty-two and sixty-five. The solid line in the figure shows the proportion of employees working at fifty who *remain* at subsequent ages. For example, only 21 percent remain until age sixty-two, only 5 percent until sixty-five.

The jumps in departure rates (at ages fifty-five, sixty, sixty-two, and sixty-five) coincide with the economic incentives in the firm's pension plan and the Social Security program. The incentive effects of defined benefit pension plans, as well as the incentive effects of Social Security, are best described by the accrual of future pension benefits. The compensation value of a firm pension plan is the incremental change (or accrual) in the present value of all future pension benefits that results from continued work. This puts pension and Social Security compensation in the same units as wage earnings. Figure 6 shows wage earnings by age, pension accrual by age, and Social Security accrual by age for a representative employee at the company. The compensation value of the plans changes discontinuously at certain specific ages.

The discontinuities in compensation correspond directly with the jumps in departure rates from the firm. The discontinuities are as follows: (1) By working until age fifty-five, the worker becomes eligible for early retirement benefits. Thus there is a large pension accrual at age fifty-five (the large spike in the graph). This leads to a large increase in retirement at age fifty-five. To understand the potential importance of the early retirement benefits, suppose that, if it were not for this inducement, the departure rates would remain at 3 percent until age sixty instead of the 11 or 12 percent rates that are observed. Departure at 3 percent a year means that 14 percent of those who were employed at fifty-five would have left before age sixty; at 11 percent a year, 44 percent would leave between ages fifty-five and fifty-nine. (2) Employees with thirty or more years of service can receive "full" unreduced retirement benefits at age sixty. The same full-benefit formula is used for retirement in every year after age sixty. For these employees, there is a sharp decrease in the compensation value of the pension plan between ages sixty and sixty-one, equivalent to a wage cut of about 14 percent. Again, there is an increase in departure rates at age sixty, corresponding to this decrease in pension accrual. (3) Although there

David A. Wise

Figure 6 Wage Earnings, Pension Accrual, and Social Security
(Accrual for representative person in firm 1)

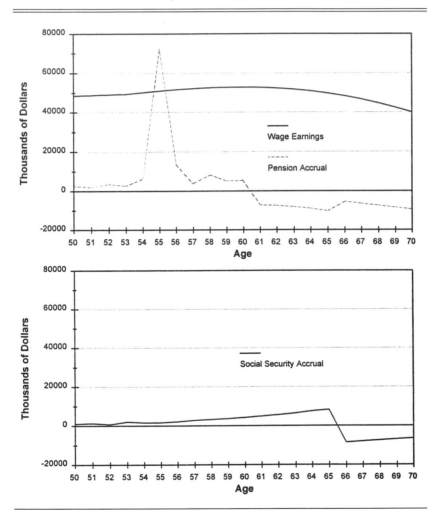

is no discontinuity in the compensation value of retirement programs at age sixty-two, workers first become eligible for Social Security benefits at age sixty-two, and this eligibility induces a jump in retirement rates. (4) Social Security accruals increase up to age sixty-five (the normal retirement age) but fall sharply thereafter. After age sixty-five,

Social Security accrual becomes negative, equivalent to about −$8,500 at age sixty-six.

To summarize: an important economic trend among older Americans has been the dramatic reduction in their labor force participation. The trend toward early retirement is especially striking when viewed in light of the increasing life expectancy and the increasing proportion of the population that is old. The prospect is a declining proportion of working people supporting an increasing proportion of retirees. In addition to this economic squeeze, economic analysis reveals that public and private pension provisions have themselves contributed to the decline in labor force participation. It seems apparent that the retirement income provided by Social Security and private pensions has allowed workers to leave the labor force at younger and younger ages and still support themselves after retirement. Indeed, a principal intent of pensions is to allow just that. But Social Security and private pension provisions do not provide for postretirement income in a neutral fashion; they provide strong incentives to remain in the labor force until some age and then typically provide strong incentive to leave at some later age, often as young as fifty-five. Put another way, they penalize work by older employees.

HEALTH STATUS AND HEALTH INSURANCE

Although increasing attention is being addressed to the incentive effects of employer-provided pension plans, much less attention has been directed to the effects of employer-provided health insurance.[6] The importance of health status on retirement is made clear in table 1, which is based on a question in the new Health and Retirement Survey that asks respondents, who were between fifty-one and sixty-one at the time of the survey, whether they believe they will be working past age

---

6. Exceptions are the papers by Madrian (1993), Phelan and Rust (1993), Gruber and Madrian (1993), and to some extent Lumsdaine, Stock, and Wise (1995).

David A. Wise

Table 1   Self-Assessment of the Probability of Working Past Age 62
                by Pension Coverage and Health Status

Employer-Provided Pension Plan	HEALTH STATUS	
	Excellent or very good	*Fair or poor*
Defined benefit	0.44	0.36
No plan	0.56	0.53

SOURCE: Calculations from HRS data. I am indebted to Kathleen McGarry for making the calculations.

sixty-two. Two features of these numbers stand out: First, the data confirm the implications of defined benefit pension plan incentives shown in figures 5 and 6, that is, that persons with such a pension plan are more likely than persons without a plan to say that they will work past age sixty-two. Second, persons who say they are in excellent or very good health are more likely than persons who say they are in fair or poor health to say they expect to work past age sixty-two. The difference is especially marked for persons with a pension plan. The effect of the pension plan is most pronounced for persons who are in poor health.

Recent interest has focused not on health status, which is a common determinant of retirement, but on the effect of employer-provided health insurance. Medicare is not available until age sixty-five. Therefore, the retirement decisions of persons with employer-provided health insurance may be influenced by whether the firm offers retirees health insurance. If not, an employee may continue to work until sixty-five to avoid a period without health insurance coverage. In contrast, an employee who is eligible for retiree health insurance may feel less economic need to continue to work; see table 2, wherein respondents are distinguished by whether they have retiree health insurance. On the basis of the self-assessments of the probability of working past sixty-two, the effect of retiree health insurance depends on health status. Persons who are in excellent or good health and have retiree health insurance are less likely than persons without such insurance to plan

Table 2 Self-Assessment of the Probability of Working Past Age 62 by Pension Coverage, Health Status, and Retiree Health Insurance

Employer-Provided Pension Plan	HEALTH STATUS	
	Excellent or very good	*Fair or poor*
With retiree health insurance		
Defined benefit	0.43	0.35
No plan	0.53	0.48
Without retiree health insurance		
Defined benefit	0.56	0.36
No plan	0.60	0.47

SOURCE: Calculations from HRS data. I am indebted to Kathleen McGarry for making the calculations.

to work past age sixty-two. The plans of persons who say they are in fair or poor health are unrelated to whether they have retiree health insurance. Persons in both health status groups, however, are much less likely to plan to work past age sixty-two if they have a defined benefit pension plan.

What Could Change Retirement Decisions?

The discussion above makes clear the strong relationship between Social Security and pension plan provisions on the one hand and employee retirement decisions on the other. How would changes in these provisions affect retirement? Here, I illustrate the likely effect of changes in Social Security and plan provisions by considering employees in a specific firm. I emphasize in particular the interaction between Social Security and pension plan provisions. The predicted effects are based on an "option value" model of retirement developed by Stock and Wise (1990a, 1990b), and the results are based on simulations of model predictions under various plan provisions.

A key component of the model is that anticipated future increases in total compensation—wage earnings, plus pension accrual, plus Social Security accrual—work to keep employees in the labor force, whereas anticipated declines in total compensation encourage employees to leave the labor force. For example, an employee who is age fifty and anticipates a large increase in accrued pension benefits at age fifty-five will be inclined to work at least until fifty-five to take advantage of the large increase in promised future pension benefits that occurs at that age. In contrast, a person who knows that the present value of future pension benefits will decline if he continues to work will be more inclined to retire. In some instances, wage earnings can be entirely offset by reductions in the present value of promised future pension and Social Security benefits. It is typical for declines in pension and Social Security accruals at older ages, added to the decline in real earnings at older ages, to produce a large decline in total compensation.

For illustration, let us consider employees in a large Fortune 500 firm who are covered by a defined benefit pension plan with normal retirement at sixty-five and early retirement at fifty-five. "Cliff vesting" (attaining entitlement to a pension) occurs at ten years of service, except that employees with fewer years of service are vested at age sixty-five. The normal retirement benefit at sixty-five depends on earnings, age, and years of service at retirement (that is, at the time of departure from the firm). A person can retire and elect to start receiving benefits before age sixty-five, but the normal benefit will be reduced by 5 percent for each year that receipt of benefits precedes age sixty-five. A person who retired at fifty-five, for example, would receive 50 percent of the normal retirement benefit of a person who left the firm at sixty-five. (The normal benefit also depends on years of service at the time of retirement.) If a person has thirty years of service at retirement, and if the person is age sixty or older, however, the person is eligible for 100 percent of the normal benefit. Benefits are reduced 5 percent for each year that retirement precedes age sixty, if the person has thirty years of service. For example, a person who retired at age fifty-five with thirty years of service would receive 75 percent of the normal benefit.[7]

The result of the simulations demonstrates first that changes in key plan provisions can have a substantial effect on retirement rates. Additional simulations show that the effect of changing Social Security provisions depends critically on whether they are accompanied by corresponding changes in the firm pension plan provisions. The results are reported relative to the retirement rates under the current pension and Social Security provisions (see table 3). The retirement rates are the proportion of employees working at age fifty who have retired by selected subsequent ages.

CHANGES IN FIRM PENSION PLAN PROVISIONS

The firm plan provides that benefits increase with years of service. But an employee who has thirty or more years of service at age sixty is eligible for 100 percent of normal retirement benefits. Continued employment will not increase benefits. Thus if the person works another year, a year of benefits is forgone, but the forgone year of benefits is not offset by an increase in benefits when the person does retire; the present value of benefits is simply lower by the amount of the annual benefit. The effect of eliminating this provision, and allowing benefits to increase with years of service above thirty years, is substantial, reducing from 41 to 29 percent the proportion of employees working at age fifty who are retired by sixty and from 64 to 46 percent the proportion retired by sixty-two.

Under the current plan in this firm, employees can begin to receive pension benefits at fifty-five, the early retirement age. Suppose that instead of fifty-five the early retirement is at age sixty. This change would reduce the proportion of employees retired at fifty-nine from 29

---

7. Other provisions are described in detail in Lumsdaine, Stock, and Wise (1994a).

David A. Wise

Table 3   Effect of Changes in Pension and Social Security Provisions on Percent Retired by Selected Ages

Change in Pension and Social Security (SS) Provisions	PERCENT RETIRED BY AGE					
	55	59	60	61	62	65
0. Current plan	7%	29%	41%	51%	64%	86%
1. Eliminate pension 30 years of service (YOS) at age 60 rule			41 to 29%	51 to 35%	64 to 46%	86 to 77%
2. Raise pension eligible-to-retire (ER) age from 55 to 60		29 to 4%				
3. Raise pension ER age from 55 to 62 and change 30 YOS at 60 rule to 30 YOS at 62				51 to 8%		86 to 74%
4. Raise SS normal retirement (NR) age from 65 to 67 and actuarially fair post-65 benefits increase						86 to 83%
5. No SS ER					64 to 57%	
6. No SS					64 to 49%	86 to 67%
7. SS changes in 4 and pension ER from 55 to 62, NR from 65 to 67, and 30 YOS rule at 62 instead of 60	7 to 4%	29 to 6%	41 to 7%	51 to 8%	64 to 32%	86 to 72%

percent to 4 percent. Under the current age early retirement age (fifty-five), few employees retire before fifty-five; if the early retirement age were raised to sixty, few employees would retire before sixty. Suppose that instead of fifty-five the early retirement age were raised to sixty-two —the same as the Social Security early retirement age—and that the thirty-year provision provided 100 percent of benefits at sixty-two instead of sixty. There would be a substantial reduction in departure rates before age sixty-two, with retirement by sixty-one reduced from 51 percent to 8 percent. Again, few employees would retire before sixty-two, the early retirement age.

The simulations emphasize that employees are unlikely to retire before retirement benefits can be received. This is consistent with the evidence that most U.S. families have limited personal financial assets on the eve of retirement and would be unable to support themselves in retirement without employer-provided pension or Social Security benefits. In general, then, the firm pension plan provisions have an important effect on retirement. The simulations below show that for persons with a firm plan such as the one considered here, changes in Social Security provisions are less important.

CHANGES IN SOCIAL SECURITY

Under current Social Security provisions, normal retirement benefits are available at age sixty-five and early retirement benefits are available at age sixty-two, with benefits actuarially reduced if they are taken between sixty-two and sixty-five. In addition benefits are increased 3 percent a year if receipt of benefits begins after sixty-five.[8] (An actuarially fair increase would be close to 7 percent.) Over the next three decades the Social Security normal retirement age is scheduled to increase from sixty-five to sixty-seven. The early Social Security normal retirement age will remain at sixty-two, but benefits will be reduced actuarially from full benefits at sixty-seven instead of sixty-five. In addition, the increase in post-sixty-five retirement benefits will be increased from 3 percent to an actuarially fair rate.

Although the retirement rates of persons over sixty is reduced, the overall effect of these proposed changes is small. The proportion of persons *employed* at sixty-two who retire at that age is reduced from 26 to 23 percent, and the age sixty-five retirement rate is reduced from 35 to 26 percent. But the percent of persons employed at age fifty who are

---

8. At the time these data were collected.

retired by sixty-five is reduced only from 86 to 83 percent, as shown under change 4 in the table. Thus compared to changes in the firm plan provisions, the effect of scheduled changes in Social Security provisions is small in this firm. Although these rates pertain to a single firm, the simulated effects would be typical of employees in firms covered by a similar defined benefit pension plan.

Even eliminating Social Security early retirement altogether would have only a modest effect on cumulative departure rates from *this* firm, reducing departures by age sixty-two from 64 percent to 57 percent. Although the retirement rate for employees age sixty-two would be reduced—from 26 percent to 18 percent—because under the current firm plan almost sixty-five percent of employees now retire by age sixty-two, the change in the retirement rate at sixty-two pertains to only a small proportion of all employees. But no Social Security benefits at all would have a much larger effect, reducing departure by sixty-five from 86 percent to 67 percent. Thus it would be inaccurate to say that Social Security doesn't matter, even in this firm with its defined benefit pension plan.

In addition, a large fraction of employees is not covered by employer-provided pension plans and relies almost exclusively on Social Security for support in retirement (see figures 4a and 4b above). For this group of employees, most of whom have virtually no personal financial asset saving as they near retirement age, an increase in the Social Security retirement age would have an enormous effect on retirement. It seems clear that most of those who now retire at sixty-two would have to remain in the labor force until the new early retirement age.

INTEGRATED CHANGES IN SOCIAL SECURITY
AND THE PENSION PLAN

If the scheduled Social Security changes are imposed and the firm provisions were changed to "correspond" to the Social Security provisions, the effects would be much like those that result if only the firm plan provisions were changed. In addition to the planned Social Security changes, consider these changes: the firm early retirement age is increased from fifty-five to sixty-two, the thirty-year provision applies at age sixty-two instead of sixty, and the firm normal retirement age is increased from sixty-five to sixty-seven. The effect of the joint changes is large, but the comparison of changes 4 and 7 in table 3 makes clear that most of the effect is due to the change in the firm plan. Retirement before sixty-two is reduced from 51 to 8 percent, the same as in change 4, which affects only the pension plan. Retirement by sixty-five is reduced from 86 to 72 percent; the reduction in change 4 is from 86 to 74 percent.

Summary and Discussion

Despite the rapid aging of the population and the increase in life expectancy, there has been a dramatic drop in the labor force participation of older Americans over the past three or four decades. The accelerated drop in labor force participation seems to correspond roughly to the introduction of Social Security and the adoption of employer-provided pension plans. I have illustrated that Social Security and employer-provided pension plans provide substantial incentive to leave the labor force early. The quantitative effect of this inducement is illustrated by the simulated effects of changes in pension plan and Social Security provisions on the retirement decisions of employees in a large firm who are covered by a typical defined benefit pension plan. Scheduled Social Security changes would have little effect on the retirement decisions of employees with such a plan. But if the pension plan provisions were changed to correspond to the Social Security changes, the effect would be large. Although apparently not contemplated by current legislation, it is also clear that an increase in the Social Security early retirement age would substantially affect the

David A. Wise

early retirement rates of the large number of employees not covered by a pension plan.

Health is also an important determinant of retirement, and the effect of health status may interact with the effect of pension plan provisions. Available data also suggest that employer-provided retiree health insurance may facilitate early retirement and that the insurance effect may in turn interact with health status and with pension plan provisions.

Personal saving cannot explain the trend toward earlier departure from the labor force. Indeed, low personal saving magnifies the pressure that population trends place on the public Social Security system. Can personal saving be increased? Based on my long-running and varied analyses with Steven Venti and James Poterba, I believe that contributions to IRAs represent an important increase in personal saving and that the saving effect of this program would have continued to grow had the program not been curtailed by the Tax Reform Act of 1986. The weight of the evidence also suggests that the 401(k) program has contributed importantly to personal saving for retirement and continues to do so.[9] The saving effect of these programs remains an important issue of economic debate, and the extent to which personal saving can be increased is critically important to future generations of older Americans and to the health of the economy in general. Current trends in population aging, earlier withdrawal from the labor force, and limited personal saving seem destined to clash.

The major reason for pension plans is to allow workers to retire with a secure source of income thereafter. Thus it should be expected, and welcomed, that increased pension coverage allows workers to retire earlier. The issue here, however, is not that the accumulation of pen-

---

9. The evidence is summarized in Poterba, Venti, and Wise (1996a) and is evaluated in more detail in Poterba, Venti, and Wise (1996b). The evidence is also critically considered by Hubbard and Skinner (1996) and by Bernheim (1996). An alternative view is presented by Engen, Gale, and Scholz (1996).

sion benefits allows retirement but rather that the typical accumulation pattern penalizes continued labor force participation of elderly workers, often imposing a substantial "wage tax" on older workers. The accumulation of pension wealth is not a neutral bystander with respect to the decision of elderly workers to continue in the labor force, but it is not the amount of the pension entitlement that is open to question. Even if the total entitlement is relatively small, the accrual pattern may mean a large bonus for remaining in the firm until some age and then a large loss from staying. At certain ages, the decision to continue working is likely to mean that a large fraction of wage earnings is offset through a loss in the value of future pension benefits. After sixty-five, this is also the case with Social Security benefits. If there is a problem with the current structure of pensions, it is that it constrains the choice of older workers to continue in the labor force. Whether this is the optimal plan structure in light of current demographic trends is open to question.

WHAT CAN BE DONE?

First, we should increase the Social Security retirement age. This is planned, but the proposed change is too far off. In my view, two changes in current employer practice should be considered also and possibly encouraged: movement from defined benefit to defined contribution plans (with the benefit determined by how much is contributed to the pension fund) and gradual, rather than abrupt, withdrawal from the labor force. In addition, private saving for retirement should be encouraged. Switching to defined contribution plans would have two major advantages. First, it would make the decision of whether to continue in the labor force a neutral one at each age. There would be no artificial incentives created by implicit subsidies and taxes on labor force participation, such as those inherent in the provisions of typical defined benefit plans. A person who worked another year would be compensated through wage earnings and through increased future

David A. Wise

pension entitlement; one would not tend to offset the other, as is typical under current plans. This is not to say that all, or even most, older workers would choose to remain longer in the labor force, but many would. Some might retire sooner. But all workers could make the choice more on the basis of personal preference and less on the basis of provisions that have the effect, sometimes unintended, of "tilting the playing field." Second, pension entitlements should be portable and transferred from one job to another with the employee. Changing jobs should not engender losses in pension entitlement, and labor mobility should not be artificially discouraged by a loss of pension benefits. To some extent, the ongoing expansion of 401(k) plans and traditional employer-provided defined contribution plans is moving in this direction.

There are, however, several potential pitfalls to such a course. Defined benefit plans may have advantages not typically associated with defined contribution plans. Defined benefit plans, for instance, may provide a graceful way of releasing older workers from the labor force. There is considerable anecdotal evidence, for example, that some universities are concerned that, with the elimination of mandatory retirement at age seventy, many faculty members will wish to work past that age. Also, employees may not choose to retire when they "should." This would not necessarily be a problem if wage earnings could be easily adjusted to reflect productivity. But it is often difficult to make such adjustments, both because of employers' desire to avoid conflict and potential morale problems and because of the risk of age discrimination lawsuits.

This suggests that switching to defined contribution plans, or in other ways limiting the incentive effects of defined benefit plans, might well be accompanied by pressures to change the age-wage profile. I think it would be a mistake to try to change one while restricting changes in the other. This problem is related to the second retirement practice issue that I believe should be addressed.

The vast majority of workers now go from full-time work to retirement overnight. Although some recent research has emphasized work after retirement, it is limited to a small proportion of retirees, is almost never at the same firm from which the employee retired, and is usually part-time and of short duration. Current institutional arrangements make gradual withdrawal from the labor force difficult. It is rare, for example, for older employees to take less responsible jobs at lower pay or for older workers to go from full-time to part-time work with the same employer. Some firms are now exploring such arrangements, and older workers would be well served by such schemes. The problem of course is not simply that firms don't want to do it but that employees are not used to such arrangements. Such changes would require adjustments in the expectations of older workers, including relinquishing higher-level jobs and accepting lower-level positions in hierarchical firms.

These arrangements are one way to equate the wage compensation of older workers with their productivity, as well as to provide an alternative that many older employees may prefer to abrupt retirement. Such arrangements would also be consistent with and facilitate adoption of defined contribution pension plans.

In addition, personal saving for retirement must be encouraged. The U.S. personal saving rate is currently the lowest of any industrialized country. Personal saving in the United States has declined substantially as a fraction of personal income since the early 1950s, and a large proportion of families reach retirement age with little or no personal saving.

In short, even though individuals are living longer *and* even though a rapidly growing fraction of the population is old, workers are at once saving less and leaving the labor force at younger and younger ages. The retired portion of the population is increasing, and the employed portion is declining. Whether by intent or happenstance, firm pension plan and Social Security provisions continue to encourage this trend. Several features of the U.S. behavior are striking. First, a large proportion of the population has virtually no personal retirement saving, other than housing equity. Social Security wealth is the primary asset of a majority of the elderly. Second, corporate pension plans, although an important form of saving for retirement, may also be the most important reason for early withdrawal from the labor force. Although the planned increase in the Social Security retirement age is intended to prolong labor force participation, and thus relieve financial pressure on that program, corporate pension plan provisions present more-powerful enticements to do the opposite. Third, empirical evidence indicates that personal saving can be affected substantially by special retirement saving programs.

These facts suggest that consideration be given to four directions for change in public and private policy: more-rapid increase in the Social Security retirement age, movement from defined benefit to defined contribution pension plans, institutional arrangements to facilitate gradual withdrawal from the labor force, and greater encouragement of personal saving for retirement through IRA and 401(k) plans. The current administration has backed away from a more rapid increase in the Social Security retirement age, and both political parties have promised to close their eyes to this critical issue; but in my view the deficit squeeze will not be solved without such a change. The administration's plans seem to contain little if any incentive for personal retirement saving, and indeed tax legislation that has evolved since 1982 may ultimately work strongly to restrict saving, as explained by John Shoven and David Wise (in this volume). Although there has been a great deal of emphasis on sacrifice, the idea that individuals must save more if the economy is to prosper and if older Americans are to be secure in retirement has gone virtually unmentioned. Important opportunities to encourage personal saving have been lost, and restrictions on saving seem to have been adopted with little concern for future economic growth and for the well-being of future elderly. Potential changes in employer retirement policies should be considered by the private sector.

References

Bernheim, Douglas. 1996 "Rethinking Saving Incentives." Manuscript, Stanford University.

Engen, Eric, William G. Gale, and John Karl Scholz. 1996. "Effects of Tax-Based Saving Incentives on Saving and Wealth: A Review of the Literature." *Journal of Economic Perspectives*. November.

Feinstein, Jonathan, and Daniel McFadden. 1989. "The Dynamics of Housing Demand by the Elderly: Wealth, Cash Flow, and Demographic Effects." In D. Wise, ed., *The Economics of Aging*. Chicago: University of Chicago Press.

Gruber, Jonathan, and Brigitte Madrian. 1993. "Health Insurance and Early Retirement: Evidence from the Availability of Continuation Coverage." Forthcoming in D. Wise, ed., *Advances in the Economics of Aging*. Chicago: University of Chicago Press.

Hubbard, R. Glenn, and Jonathan S. Skinner. 1996. "The Effectiveness of Saving Incentives: A Review of the Evidence." *Journal of Economic Perspectives*. November.

Kotlikoff, Laurence J., and David A. Wise. 1987. "The Incentive Effects of Private Pension Plans." In Z. Bodie, J. Shoven, and D. Wise, eds., *Issues in Pension Economics*. Chicago: University of Chicago Press.

———. 1988. "Pension Backloading, Wage Taxes, and Work Disincentives." In L. Summers, ed., *Tax Policy and the Economy*. Vol. 2. Cambridge, Mass.: MIT Press.

———. 1989a. "Employee Retirement and a Firm's Pension Plan." In D. Wise, ed., *The Economics of Aging*. Chicago: University of Chicago Press.

———. 1989b. *The Wage Carrot and the Pension Stick*. Kalamazoo, Mich.: W. E. Upjohn Institute for Employment Research.

Lumsdaine, Robin L., James H. Stock, and David A. Wise. 1990. "Efficient Windows and Labor Force Reduction." *Journal of Public Economics* 43: 131–59.

———. 1991. "Windows and Retirement." *Annales d'Economie et de Statistique* 20/21: 219–42.

———. 1992. "Three Models of Retirement: Computational Complexity versus Predictive Validity." In D. Wise, ed., *Topics in the Economics of Aging*. Chicago: University of Chicago Press.

———. 1994a. "Pension Plan Provisions and Retirement: Men and Women, Medicare, and Models." In D. Wise, ed., *Studies in the Economics of Aging.* Chicago: University of Chicago Press.

———. 1994b. "Retirement Incentives: The Interaction between Employer-Provided Pension Plans, Social Security, and Retiree Health Benefits." National Bureau of Economic Research (NBER) working paper #4613, January. Forthcoming in NBER-Japan Center for Economic Research conference volume. Chicago: University of Chicago Press.

———. 1995. "Why are Retirement Rates So High at Age 65?" NBER working paper #5190, July. Forthcoming in D. Wise, ed., *Advances in the Economics of Aging.* Chicago: University of Chicago Press.

Madrian, Brigitte C. 1993. "Post-Retirement Health Insurance and the Decision to Retire." Manuscript, Department of Economics, MIT.

Phelan, Christopher, and John P. Rust. 1993. "How Social Security and Medicare Affect Retirement Behavior in a World of Incomplete Markets." Manuscript, Department of Economics, University of Wisconsin.

Poterba, James M., Steven F. Venti, and David A. Wise. 1996a. "How Retirement Saving Programs Increase Saving." *Journal of Economic Perspectives.* November.

———. 1996b. "Personal Retirement Saving Programs and Asset Accumulation: Reconciling the Evidence." NBER working paper, May.

Ransom, Roger L., and Richard Sutch. 1988. "The Decline of Retirement and the Rise of Efficiency Wages: U.S. Retirement Patterns, 1870–1940." In R. Ricardo-Campbell and E. Lazear, eds., *Issues in Contemporary Retirement.* Stanford: Hoover Institution.

Sandefur, Gary D., and Nancy Brandon Tuma. 1987. "Social and Economic Trends among the Aged in the United States, 1940–1985." Mimeo, Hoover Institution.

Sheiner, Louise, and David N. Weil. 1992. "The Housing Wealth of the Aged." NBER working paper #4115.

Stock, James H., and David A. Wise. 1990a. "Pensions, the Option Value of Work, and Retirement." *Econometrica* 58, no. 5 (September): 1151–80.

———. 1990b. "The Pension Inducement to Retire: An Option Value Analysis." In D. Wise, ed., *Issues in the Economics of Aging.* Chicago: University of Chicago Press.

Venti, Steven F., and David A. Wise. 1989. "Aging, Moving, and Housing Wealth." In Wise, ed., *Economics of Aging.* Chicago: University of Chicago Press.

———. 1990. "But They Don't Want to Reduce Housing Equity." In Wise, ed., *Issues in the Economics of Aging*. Chicago: University of Chicago Press.

———. 1991. "Aging and the Income Value of Housing Wealth." *Journal of Public Economics* 44: 371–97.

Wise, David A. 1997. "Retirement against the Demographic Trend: More Older People Living Longer, Working Less, and Saving Less." *Demography* 34, no. 1 (February): 83–95.

The Adequacy of
Personal Retirement Saving
Issues and Options

When the baby boom generation retires, an unprecedented fraction of the U.S. adult population will be out of the labor force, acting as net consumers of social resources. This observation raises a fundamental long-run policy question: who will pay for these resources? There are four possibilities. The first is that no one pays—the baby boomers could simply accept much lower standards of living during retirement or continue to work indefinitely. Second, the government could provide generous benefits through Social Security. Third, employers could accumulate substantial stocks of wealth on behalf of workers through pension plans. Fourth, each household could save aggressively on its own behalf.

The first possibility is far-fetched. Historically, the elderly have wielded considerable political clout and have used this clout to protect their economic interests. The political power of the elderly can only expand with their ranks. While the baby boomers might tolerate incremental increases in the age of retirement, they will probably resist more drastic measures. The second possibility flies in the face of fiscal reality. To maintain existing Social Security benefits (including Medicare), the government would need to impose burdensome taxes on younger generations. Although the working-age population is generally less politically active than retirees, huge tax increases would probably have a galvanizing effect, polarizing the political system along generational lines. The third possibility is relevant for a declining fraction of workers. With the increasing popularity of participant-controlled, defined contribution plans (like 401(k)s and 403(b)s), pensions are becoming indistinguishable from other forms of voluntary personal saving. Finally, the financial behavior of baby boomers to date has been inconsistent with the fourth possibility.

Obviously, something has to give. The question before us is whether far-sighted public policy can resolve this problem in a constructive way. If nothing is done, it could lead to intergenerational warfare over public retirement benefits and other entitlements. If, in contrast, the baby boomers could be induced to save more for their own retirements, this would reduce the pressures that are likely to produce conflict and crisis.

In this chapter, I review the factors that are contributing to the problem of paying for retirement in the twenty-first century and discuss policy alternatives, including proposals to encourage greater personal saving.

The Growing Importance of Personal Retirement Saving

Over the next few decades, new retirees will probably become increasingly reliant on voluntary personal saving to achieve retirement income security. This forecast reflects two concerns: first, that the costs of retirement will rise steadily and, second, that households will find it increasingly difficult to meet these costs through alternatives to personal saving. I will elaborate on each of these points in turn.

D. Douglas Bernheim

TRENDS IN THE COSTS OF RETIREMENT

Let us begin this discussion by exploring briefly what we might mean by the phrase *costs of retirement*. One possibility is to limit the discussion of costs to necessities, such as basic nutrition, shelter, clothing, and medical care; this requires us to draw a distinction between purchases that arise from need and purchases that arise from preference. Of course, needs vary in intensity, and they are often difficult to distinguish from desires. Ultimately, it is difficult to draw a line between necessities and luxuries based on objective standards. Perhaps more important, retirement itself is usually a reflection of preferences. Except in cases where disabilities limit activity, individuals could continue to work long after they actually retire. To put it somewhat differently, it is difficult to make the case that retirement leisure time is a necessity.

At the opposite extreme is the view that the costs of retirement should be defined to include whatever retirees choose to spend their money on. But this view quickly leads to the tautology that expenditures are always just sufficient to cover costs. From this perspective, one cannot meaningfully raise, let alone address, issues concerning the adequacy of retirement income.

An intermediate possibility—and the one adopted in this chapter—is to define the costs of retirement relative to preretirement expectations. If a healthy woman expects to retire at age sixty-two, to remain in and maintain her existing house, to have good medical care, to eat well both at home and at restaurants, to take yearly vacations, to play golf weekly, and so forth, then these expectations determine her perceived cost of retirement.[1] If, as is commonly assumed in economic analyses of retirement, individuals have perfect foresight, then reality will always match expectations, and this third approach will be equiv-

---

1. Naturally, for this purpose, one must be careful to distinguish between serious expectations and fantasies, such as winning the lottery and living out one's days in the lap of luxury.

alent to the second (wherein expenditures always match costs and the notion of "saving adequacy" is ill-defined). However, if individuals lack perfect foresight, then reality may frustrate (or surpass) expectations. Individuals may regret having saved too little (or too much). In that case, the shortfall between expectations and reality provides a natural benchmark by which to measure the adequacy of retirement income.

The appeal of this final perspective is practical as well as theoretical. The influential political activities of the elderly are shaped by their *perceived* needs and by the gap between their expectations and reality, rather than by any objective notion of need. These political activities will become increasingly influential with the aging of the baby boomers, as the elderly come to account for a rising fraction of the population. Economic analysis must either inform the public policy debate from a perspective that is relevant to the affected interest groups or risk being dismissed as having no bearing on the issues of concern.

One important driver of retirement costs is the length of the retirement period. Historically, this period has expanded on both ends, as workers have retired earlier and lived longer. There is as yet no indication that the trend toward earlier retirement will reverse; indeed, a recent Merrill Lynch survey revealed that the typical baby boomer expects to retire at age sixty-two. At the same time, there is every indication that the baby boomers will live significantly longer than their parents. Even official mortality projections, which envision significant gains in life expectancy, may significantly understate the longevity of those retiring in the next century. According to Vaupel (1992), "If current rates of progress in reducing mortality at advanced ages continue or accelerate, children alive today may live 90 or even 100 years on average."

Longer life reflects better health. This does not imply, however, that the costs of medical care will decline, for medical expenses rise sharply during the last few years of life (Cutler et al. 1990). Increased longevity may simply defer the infirmities that give rise to these hefty expenses. Medical costs may also rise with the development of new technologies and procedures, particularly if these developments prolong the final stages of infirmity. The aging of the baby boom generation will also increase the per capita demand for medical services, which should place upward pressure on the costs of medical care.

This final point illustrates a more general concern. Elderly individuals tend to consume a systematically different bundle of goods (medical care, houses in Florida, ocean cruises, etc.) than younger individuals. As the composition of the population shifts toward the elderly, the per capita demand for these services will rise. For goods and services with sufficiently large, long-run supply elasticities, the resulting impact on relative prices should be low. In instances where resources are inherently limited (e.g., desirable homesites or vacation locations), however, one would expect relative prices to rise. In effect, the baby boomers will bid against one another for scarce resources that are desirable complements to retirement activities, just as they set off a sharp rise in housing prices during the 1980s by bidding against one another for homes.

Improved health also has implications for the nonmedical cost of living during retirement. A long-standing debate is whether retirees must spend more or less than younger workers to achieve a similar standard of living. To a large extent, this debate turns on the issue of whether spending is a complement to or substitute for retirement leisure time. The case for complementarity is strongest for healthy retirees, who often seek to fill their leisure time with costly activities (e.g., travel, golf). In contrast, nonmedical expenses may fall for infirm retirees who find themselves less able to enjoy active lifestyles.[2] As the average retiree becomes healthier, one would expect to observe a greater perceived need for spendable income.

There is also reason to believe that the elderly form perceptions of needs during retirement with reference to their own accustomed stan-

---

2. Naturally, nonmedical expenses may rise for those who need help with household activities as a result of disabilities.

dards of living. That is, they wish to avoid significant declines in their living standards after retirement. To the extent the country experiences rising standards of living generally, one would therefore expect the perceived costs of retirement to rise commensurately.

ALTERNATIVES TO PERSONAL SAVING

Financial planners commonly compare retirement planning to the construction of a three-legged stool, where the legs represent Social Security, private pensions, and personal savings. To this stool one might add one final leg: the possibility of receiving inheritances from previous generations. Once one has evaluated the costs of retirement (as defined above), one can assess the need for personal saving by evaluating the size and integrity of the other legs.

Social Security and Medicare

The aging of the baby boom generation is cause for considerable concern about the future of Social Security and Medicare. Today, the elderly represent about 12 percent of the U.S. population. That figure will rise to 20 percent by the year 2029, when the youngest boomers reach age sixty-five. Today, there are roughly 3.2 workers for each Social Security beneficiary. It is expected that, by 2029, there will be only 2.1 workers for each Social Security beneficiary. If the government were to follow its historical practice of financing contemporaneous benefits for retirees on a "pay-as-you-go" basis, the implied tax increase on younger generations would be enormous.

Although current policy strives to shift some of this burden back to the baby boomers by forcing them to contribute to the accumulation of a substantial resources in the Social Security trust fund, projected trust fund balances will not be sufficient to cover benefits under current statutes. According to the Social Security Administration (SSA), a relatively modest increase in payroll taxes—on the order of 2 to 4 percentage points—is required to redress the imbalance in Old Age, Survivors, and Disability Insurance (OASDI). Unfortunately, OASDI is only one part of the problem. Medicare in particular will contribute even more to the fiscal shortfall in the next century. Moreover, these figures presuppose immediate action. If payroll tax increases are delayed, more drastic action will be required. And since the ultimate crisis is still relatively far off in time, the prospects for rapid action appear minimal. Finally, even the SSA's pessimistic scenarios are based on potentially optimistic assumptions (e.g., concerning gains in life expectancy).

Auerbach and Kotlikoff (1994, 1995) have conducted a comprehensive study of the long-run outlook for U.S. fiscal policy and concluded that existing statutes place the country on an unsustainable path. To meet its promises in the next century, the government will need to spend trillions of dollars more than it currently expects to take in.

According to Auerbach and Kotlikoff, restoring fiscal balance requires drastic action. For example, it would take a permanent 32 percent increase in income taxes or a 29 percent decrease in all public retirement benefits (including health benefits), effective immediately. If we wait fifteen years before addressing the crisis, it would take a permanent 63 percent increase in income taxes or a 49 percent cut in retirement benefits.

Some people remain confident in Social Security because they doubt that benefit cuts will ever become politically feasible. There is little basis for this confidence. Congress has already found a number of politically acceptable ways to cut benefits. For example, during the 1980s, it delayed cost-of-living adjustments, subjected Social Security benefits to taxation, and scheduled increases in the age of normal retirement (which is equivalent to a reduction in benefits at each retirement age). If Congress faced up to the necessity of cutting benefits today, it could minimize the impact on those who have the least opportunity to adjust by scheduling larger benefit reductions for those who will retire in the more distant future (e.g., by scheduling further increases in the age of normal retirement and increases in the age of early retirement). It is more likely, however, that Congress will instead postpone the inevitable and scramble to find the least politically repugnant form of benefit cut when the crisis fully materializes. Means testing is one obvious possibility. One can easily imagine that wealth or income tests or both that exclude the wealthy will receive widespread support. Once instituted, however, such a provision would likely be used to reduce or eliminate benefits for an increasing number of Americans as the crisis worsens.

Even if Social Security benefits are not cut, it is important to realize that the fraction of preretirement household income replaced by Social Security will probably decline over the next few decades because two-earner households are much more common among the baby boomers than among their parents. Since single-earner households have historically received significant windfalls from Social Security in the form of spousal benefits, Social Security replaces a smaller fraction of preretirement earnings for two-earner households.

Private Retirement Benefits

Unlike Social Security, eligibility for private pensions is far from universal. Between 1979 and 1993, the percentage of full-time male private-sector employees participating in a pension plan fell from 55 to 51 percent. The decline was particularly striking for younger workers. Only 41 percent of full-time male private-sector employees between the ages of twenty-five and twenty-nine were covered by private pensions in 1993, compared with 53 percent in 1979 (Papke 1996). To some extent, these trends have been offset by increases in coverage for women. Many explanations have been offered for falling pension coverage, including declining marginal tax rates (Reagan and Turner 1995), falling unionization (Bloom and Freeman 1992), competitively driven cost-cutting measures, and so forth. Irrespective of the cause, the ultimate consequence will be to reduce the fraction of Americans who can rely on private pensions as a significant source of postretirement income.

The characteristics of private pensions have also been changing. Between 1985 and 1992, the number of participants in large (more than one hundred participants) defined benefit plans fell from 21.6 million to 19.8 million, while the number of participants in large defined contribution plans rose from 27.0 million to 29.5 million (Papke 1996). More specifically, the share of total pension contributions accounted for by 401(k) plans rose from 18 percent in 1985 to almost 50 percent in 1992 (U.S. Department of Labor 1996).

This shift from defined benefit to defined contribution pension plans has complex implications for retirement income security. On the one hand, defined contribution plans are fully portable, whereas the value of defined benefit pension entitlements is eroded by job mobility. On the other hand, many defined contribution plans (particularly 401(k)s) offer employees a wide range of choices, including how much to contribute, what to invest in, whether to make early withdrawals, and even whether to participate in the first place. Many employees choose to contribute little or nothing at all or withdraw their balances when they switch jobs. Many invest heavily in safe, low-return, fixed-income funds. As a result, less than one-third of pension plan sponsors believe that their employees will accumulate adequate plan balances.[3]

To state this final issue somewhat differently, the decline of defined benefit pension plans and the growth of participant-controlled plans (such as 401(k)s) has blurred the distinction between private pensions and voluntary personal saving. In effect, for many Americans, two legs have migrated around the circumference of the retirement income stool and merged into one.

---

3. Ellen E. Shultz, "Executives See Trouble in Employee's Nest Eggs," *Wall Street Journal*, March 27, 1996, p. C1. The article references a recently released survey of 520 plan sponsors, conducted by RogersCasy, a pension-consulting firm.

Intergenerational Transfers

Although precise numbers are the subject of ongoing debate (see, e.g., Kotlikoff and Summers 1988 and Modigliani 1988), there is strong evidence that, in the aggregate, substantial wealth passes between generations through gifts and bequests. Consequently, intergenerational transfers represent yet another possible source of funds to finance living expenses during retirement.

Looking to the future, the importance of intergenerational transfers is tempered by several factors. First, and perhaps most important, bequests are highly concentrated. The typical member of any generation receives next to nothing. There is little reason to believe that future beneficiaries will be any different in this respect. Second, testators are likely to live much longer than their predecessors. In the process, they may well exhaust all or most of their resources, either through normal living expenses or through large end-of-life expenses, such as nursing home care. Third, in comparison with previous generations, the current generation of elderly individuals holds a larger fraction of its wealth in forms that are not bequeathable. For example, annuities, such as Social Security or corporate pensions, generally cannot be passed on to children. According to Auerbach, Kotlikoff, and Weil (1992), the increasing annuitization of the elderly has already reduced the flow of aggregate bequests to children and grandchildren by 20 percent. Fourth, since the parents of the baby boomers, by definition, had more children per family than other generations, their bequests will be divided among a larger number of heirs. In short, a small number of baby boomers can count on inheritances to bail them out; the rest would be foolish to do so.

In one recent study, Avery and Rendall (1993) forecast aggregate bequests to baby boomers of $10.4 trillion (1989 dollars) in 115 million bequests. This implies an average bequest of $90,167. For the typical family, $90,167 would defray a nontrivial portion of the costs of retirement. It is important to keep in mind, however, that this figure is a mean, not a median. The distribution of wealth is highly skewed as a result of a relatively small number of very wealthy households. Moreover, the distribution of bequests, of necessity, closely resembles the distribution of wealth. As a result, the mean bequest significantly overstates the likely inheritance of the typical household.

Unfortunately, Avery and Rendall do not report medians or other quantiles.[4] Given their method for forecasting bequests, however, the relation between the means and medians of bequests should be similar to the relation between the means and medians of net worth. Kennickell and Shack-Marquez (1992) report that median net worth in the 1989 Survey of Consumer Finances was $47,200, compared with mean net worth of $183,700. The ratio of median-to-mean net worth is therefore 0.257. If we assume that the same relationship between means and medians holds for bequests, then the Avery-Rendall figures imply a median bequest of only $23,170.

In addition, the Avery-Rendall figures must be interpreted in light of their assumptions, which tend to overstate the magnitude of bequests. In particular, they

- Make no allowance for the likelihood of significant end-of-life expenses, such as extended nursing home care. In practice, these expenses will probably deplete a significant fraction of the wealth held by the baby boomers' parents. In fact, many individuals may exhaust their assets intentionally so that Medicaid will cover nursing home expenses (see Levin 1995).

- Use the Bureau of the Census's middle series for male and female single-year age-specific survival probabilities, forecasted for the year 2005. As mentioned above, these figures may understate improvements in longevity (Vaupel 1992). In addition, Avery and Rendall do not compensate for the fact that mortality

---

4. Instead, they examine the distribution of bequests and inheritances by reporting log-means and log-variances, which are difficult to interpret.

probabilities are correlated with wealth. Since wealthy people tend to live longer, the Avery-Rendall calculations tend to overstate bequests.

- Forecast the evolution of bequeathable assets for the baby boomers' parents using age-wealth profiles estimated from cross-sectional data, but cross-sectional estimates tend to understate significantly the rate at which the elderly deplete their resources (see Bernheim 1987).

- Assume that the baby boomers will ultimately inherit all of their parents' remaining wealth. In practice, other parties (relatives, churches, charitable foundations, and so forth) may also receive significant bequests.

In light of these considerations, even the $23,170 figure reported above probably exaggerates the likely inheritance for the typical baby boomer.

The Adequacy of Personal Saving

Economists and policymakers have, for some time, been alarmed by steep declines in rates of saving for the U.S. economy. During the 1950s and 1960s, the rate of national saving averaged more than 9 percent. It declined slightly during the 1970s and then plummeted to an average of just over 4 percent in the 1980s. For 1992, the rate of national saving stood at just 2.2 percent. As a fraction of disposable income, personal saving peaked at 9 percent in 1973 but declined to barely more than 4 percent in 1993 and 1994. Coupled with the rising costs of retirement and the probable decline in other sources of retirement income, these developments raise considerable concerns about the living standards of future retirees. In this section, I evaluate the adequacy of personal saving from two different perspectives.

ADEQUACY RELATIVE TO EXPECTATIONS

To evaluate the adequacy of saving relative to expectations, we first need to investigate the nature of expectations. Economic theory suggests that households attempt to smooth their expenditures over time to achieve a stable standard of living. If this is correct, then preretirement living standards provide the appropriate benchmark for expectations, which is confirmed by survey evidence. Nearly 40 percent of baby boomers say they expect their standard of living during retirement to be the same as before retirement, and virtually identical fractions expect better (31.2 percent) or worse (31.1 percent) standards of living. Remarkably, even among those with the lowest levels of accumulated wealth, more than 60 percent say that they expect their living standards during retirement to be as high or higher than before retirement (Bernheim 1995a).

For most individuals, the expectation of maintaining current living standards appears to include retaining their existing owner-occupied homes. One survey by the American Association of Retired Persons (AARP) found that 84 percent of persons fifty-five and over plan to stay in their homes and never move. Fully 62 percent of baby boomers say they intend to stay in a house of equal or greater value after retirement. Sixty percent regard home equity as a source of security to be used only in the event of a major emergency; 23 percent plan to pass their homes to their children through their estates; and only 14 percent intend to use home equity to finance living expenses in retirement (Bernheim 1995b). The behavior of current retirees is consistent with these statements. The elderly have proven reluctant to draw down the equity in their homes to pay for retirement, except to some extent in advanced age, when infirmities become more common (Venti and Wise 1989, 1990 and Sheiner and Weil 1992). Reverse annuity mortgages, which in principle permit households to access their home equity without moving, have proven unpopular.

In a series of studies, Bernheim (1993, 1994, 1995b, 1996a) has examined the adequacy of saving by members of the baby boom generation, under the assumptions that these individuals expect to remain in their existing houses and to smooth their standards of living through retirement. These studies consistently find that baby boomers are saving at 33 to 38 percent of the rate required to cover their expected costs of retirement.

Bernheim's analysis is based on a computer simulation model that calculates how much baby boom households with varying characteristics need to save throughout their adult lives to accumulate enough for retirement at age sixty-five. The model accounts for probable economic developments over the course of a lifetime and takes account of Social Security, private pensions, taxes, interest rates, inflation, economic growth, family composition, and employment prospects. It then compares savings prescriptions generated by the model with actual saving, which is deduced from yearly surveys that typically cover more than two thousand baby boom households.[5]

Bernheim's studies ignore a number of the factors (discussed above) that are expected to widen the gap between retirement costs and available resources. For example, they assume that baby boomers will probably live only as long as current retirees, that taxes won't rise in the future, that Social Security and other retirement benefits won't decline, and that health care costs won't rise. Thus, the savings gap is probably wider than is indicated by Bernheim's base-case calculations. Under more realistic assumptions about the future of Social Security, Bernheim (1996) finds that baby boomers are saving at only 22 percent

---

5. The data were collected through telephone interviews. To achieve a high level of compliance and to assure accuracy, questions on demographics, assets, and economic status were deferred until the end of the survey, following a lengthy series of less-personal questions. This permitted interviewers to establish credibility, to place respondents at greater ease, and to engage respondents in dialogue before posing questions of an invasive nature. As a result, response rates on financial questions were extremely high, and comparisons with data contained in the Survey of Consumer Finances reveal no indication that the key economic variables were either underreported or over-reported.

of the rate required to cover the expected costs of retirement; in a worst-case scenario (the elimination of Social Security), this figure falls to 12 percent.

A separate study conducted by Arthur D. Little and the WEFA group (originally, Wharton Economic Forecasting Associates; in 1987 it merged with Chase Econometrics but kept the acronym) reached similar conclusions (Arthur D. Little, Inc., 1993). For this study, income needed at retirement was defined as 70 percent of the average of an individual's income in the final five years in the labor force. Although this standard is somewhat ad hoc, it is a common rule of thumb used by financial planners, and it delivers on average a standard of living during retirement that is roughly comparable with that enjoyed before retirement. The Arthur D. Little—WEFA study also considers economic projections, demographic trends, and data on household financial behavior. It concludes that households without pension plans typically will have 20–30 percent of what they need to retire and that those with pension plans typically will have 50–60 percent of what they need to retire comfortably.

ADEQUACY RELATIVE TO PREVIOUS GENERATIONS

Even if future retirees do not fare as well as they expect, they may still achieve standards of living that are reasonably high by other criteria. One natural question is whether future retirees are currently saving as much as did current retirees at comparable ages. Since future retirees will probably have, on average, higher lifetime earnings than past retirees, this standard is less demanding than the one considered in the previous section.

As a practical matter, future retirees will be more concerned with their own expectations than with comparisons between themselves and previous generations. Consequently, the political system is not likely to recognize this alternative standard as relevant when the retirement crisis materializes in the next century. An investigation based on this standard, however, does provide a more complete picture of the saving problem.

Before discussing the evidence on intergenerational comparisons, it is important to settle some issues of interpretation. If one finds that younger generations are saving as much as older generations, is this a good thing or a bad thing? To answer this question, one must take the following considerations into account.

First, as discussed earlier, the costs of retirement are rising while alternatives to personal saving are declining. Among other things, retirees are living longer and more active lives, health care is becoming more expensive, cuts in Social Security benefits are likely, and traditional compulsory pensions (particularly defined benefit plans) are on the decline.

Second, the experience of elderly individuals demonstrates that, in the past, a large fraction of the population did a relatively poor job of preparing themselves for retirement. That is, even current retirees experienced a "savings gap." According to Diamond (1977), during the 1960s, some 40 percent of couples and more than 50 percent of unmarried individuals reported that they received no money income from assets after retirement. At age sixty, nearly 30 percent of middle-class individuals lacked sufficient wealth to replace two years' worth of income. Likewise, according to Hamermesh (1984), during the 1970s, most elderly individuals had not accumulated sufficient resources to sustain their accustomed standard of living. Hamermesh concluded that consumption shortly after retirement exceeded the highest sustainable level of consumption by an average of 14 percent. This study also found that most retirees were forced to reduce their expenditures substantially within a few years of retirement. Although Kotlikoff, Spivak, and Summers (1982) reached more optimistic conclusions concerning the adequacy of saving by current retirees, they attributed their findings to a fortuitous and unexpected expansion of the Social Security system (see also Hurd 1993).

Third, even if younger individuals are currently saving as much as their predecessors at comparable ages, this does not mean that they will have as much wealth at retirement. Indeed, the following factors suggest that they could end up with significantly less:

- When the baby boomers start to retire, the liquidation of assets in private portfolios, pension plans, and the Social Security trust fund could drive down asset values (see Schieber and Shoven 1994). The same investments may therefore produce less wealth at and during retirement.

- A similar point applies to housing wealth. The parents of the baby boomers earned substantial windfalls from their homes as a result of the sharp rise in real housing prices during the 1980s. If the boomers do attempt to finance their retirement spending in part by downsizing their homes, then the same demographic trends will drive real housing prices down (see Mankiw and Weil 1989).

- During the 1970s and early 1980s, real liabilities associated with fixed-rate mortgages declined sharply due to a period of high inflation. It is doubtful that inflation will significantly erode the value of the baby boomers' liabilities. Even if we experience a return to high inflation, many baby boomers have opted for adjustable-rate mortgages.

- Baby boomers are having children later than their parents did. As a result, they will have fewer years to save after the child-rearing years are over. Even if they are currently on track to match their parents' accumulations, they will probably fall behind once they reach their parents' post-child-rearing ages. Baby boomers are also having fewer children than their parents. This implies that children are currently less of a drain on their incomes and that, consequently, the end of child rearing will have a less salutary effect on their ability to save.

- Baby boomers will exhaust a larger fraction of their wealth sending their children to college both because their children are more likely to attend college and because the real costs of college have risen. This consideration may be offset to some extent by the fact that baby boomers are having fewer children than their parents.

- Baby boomers are experiencing less real wage growth than their parents did. This means that they may find it more difficult than their parents to save more as they get older. Even if they are currently keeping pace with their parents, they could soon fall behind.

For these reasons, the benchmark implicit in a comparison between baby boomers and older generations is most appropriately interpreted as reflecting a standard of inadequacy, rather than as a standard of adequacy. If the boomers are saving no more than their predecessors, they will probably be significantly worse off than a group that, on average, has not fared particularly well during retirement.

The evidence shows that the oldest cohorts achieving adulthood after the Great Depression were significantly less frugal at comparable ages than their depression-era cohorts. For example, Attanasio (1993) found a steep decline in age-specific saving rates for those born between 1925 and 1940 (similar findings appear in Bosworth, Burtless, and Sabelhaus 1991). These cohorts preceded the baby boom generation and include the parents of many baby boomers. All else equal, one would expect the retirement prospects for these cohorts to be significantly worse than for the depression-era cohorts. Note that the typical individual retiring in the 1960s, and many of those retiring in the 1970s, experienced the Great Depression as an adult. The inadequacy of saving among members of these groups (see above) bodes ill for the generations that follow.

The Congressional Budget Office (CBO) (1993) provides a comprehensive analysis of income and assets for baby boomers in 1989, and for individuals of similar ages in 1962, using the corresponding waves of the Survey of Consumer Finances. The CBO finds that baby boomers have higher real incomes than their parents did at similar ages and that, relative to income, baby boomers have at least as much wealth as their parents. Specifically, the median value of the ratio of wealth to income for thirty-five- to forty-four-year-olds was 1.23 in 1989, compared with 1.19 in 1962.

A separate study by Bernheim, Lemke, and Scholz (1997) uses the 1983, 1986, 1989, 1992, and 1995 waves of the Survey of Consumer Finances to construct age-wealth accumulation paths for successive cohorts. This study finds no upward shift in savings across cohorts. Like the generations that preceded them, typical baby boomers are on track to accumulate roughly $20,000 per capita in financial assets (including specialized accounts such as individual retirement accounts and 401(k)s) by retirement.

The findings of Bernheim, Lemke, and Scholz are less encouraging than those of the CBO. The two surveys used in the CBO study, however, were taken twenty-seven years apart and differ in variety of important respects. The CBO's findings must be interpreted in light of these differences; it is not at all clear that the CBO has compared apples to apples. For example, in 1962, the Survey of Consumer Finances reported roughly 85 percent of the assets tallied in the Federal Reserve's Flow of Funds data. In contrast, in 1989, assets in the Survey of Consumer Finances roughly equaled the Flow of Funds tally. Among the many potential explanations for this difference is that respondents have become more forthcoming about their assets, perhaps due to the advent of the "information age." Another possibility is that the ascendance of materialistic norms during the 1980s led more households to acknowledge or exaggerate their resources. To illustrate the importance of this consideration, one can adjust the CBO numbers by "benchmarking" the 1962 and 1989 surveys to the Flow of Funds data. With this adjustment, the data indicate that median wealth-to-income ratios have fallen from 1.40 in 1962 to 1.23 in 1989—a decline of more than 12 percent.

Also, the CBO's measures of wealth (which are used to calculate the wealth-to-income ratios mentioned above) include equity in homes. The inclusion or exclusion of housing wealth is significant since housing is a larger fraction of net wealth for the baby boomers than for their parents. Indeed, according to the CBO's unadjusted figures, the ratio of median nonhousing wealth to median income among thirty-five- to forty-four-year-olds is approximately 7 percent *lower* for the baby boomers than for their parents.[6]

Consequently, on the basis of the existing evidence, there is little reason to believe that the living standards of future retirees will surpass those of current retirees and considerable reason to be concerned that they may be significantly lower.

Policy Options

Discussions of potential policy responses to the U.S. saving problem typically focus on tax incentives. Although the tax system does provide the government with some tools for influencing behavior, other strategies are also available. In the next section, I attempt to address a wide range of alternatives.

TAX INCENTIVES

Concerns over low rates of saving have prompted a variety of proposals designed to stimulate saving through tax incentives, ranging from narrowly focused tax-favored savings accounts to broad-based consumption taxation. The extensive literature evaluating the effects of these measures has been the subject of several recent review articles

---

6. Author's calculations, based on figures appearing in table 4 of the CBO (1993).

(Poterba, Venti, and Wise 1996; Hubbard and Skinner 1996; and Engen, Gale, and Scholz 1996). In my own survey article (Bernheim 1996b), I draw the following conclusions from the available evidence.

First, there is little reason to believe that households increase their saving significantly in response to a *generic* increase in the after-tax rate of return. Since the evidence is poor, there is still considerable uncertainty on this point; however, it is difficult to identify any robust empirical pattern that suggests a high elasticity.

Second, the literature on the relation between individual retirement accounts (IRAs) and personal saving is inconclusive. Studies that point to a large effect on personal saving contain identifiable biases that overstate this effect, and studies that find little or no impact contain identifiable biases that understate the effect. Owing to the nature of the IRA program and the characteristics of the available data, a resolution of the IRA controversy seems unlikely.

Third, the available evidence on 401(k)s allows one to conclude with moderate confidence that, all else equal, eligibility for a 401(k) plan significantly stimulates personal saving. Econometric identification of this effect is facilitated by the fact that, in contrast to IRAs, there is considerable variation in 401(k) eligibility across the population and that some of this variation probably originates from exogenous sources. Although no existing study corresponds to the ideal statistical experiment, at least one reasonable procedure points to a substantial behavioral response despite factors that bias the findings in the opposite direction.

The apparent success of 401(k)s may be attributable to any of a number of distinguishing characteristics. Since 401(k) contribution limits are much higher than those of IRAs, they are less likely to bind. As a result, 401(k)s can increase the marginal after-tax rate of return for a much larger set of households, an effect that is often reinforced through provisions whereby employers match employee contributions. The structure of a 401(k) plan also effectively capitalizes on the psychology of saving. Since contributions occur through regular payroll deductions rather than through discretionary deposits, 401(k)s are more conducive to self-discipline. Higher contribution limits may also provide authoritative validation for higher saving targets. Since 401(k)s are organized around the workplace, they may also create positive spill-overs between employees (e.g., through informal conversations). Finally, the existence of 401(k)s has promoted the growth of retirement education in the workplace (Bernheim and Garrett 1996; Bayer, Bernheim, and Scholz 1996).

EDUCATION AND PROMOTIONAL ACTIVITY

Why do many Americans make poor financial decisions to begin with? One possibility is that they do not have the training, skill, or guidance or all three to recognize financial vulnerabilities and to formulate prudent plans (Bernheim 1995a, 1996c). If so, then education may be a powerful tool for stimulating rates of saving. This possibility has led the Department of Labor to launch a "national pension education program aimed at drawing the attention of American workers to the importance of taking personal responsibility for their retirement security" (Berg 1995, 2). The desire to shape behavior through education is also presumably behind the recent explosion of retirement education in the workplace. As of 1994, 88 percent of large employers offered some form of financial education; more than two-thirds of these added such programs after 1990.[7]

Anecdotal evidence from Japan provides some insight into the effects of promotional campaigns (Central Council for Saving Promotion 1981) in that the Japanese government launched such a campaign after World War II. To orchestrate the prosaving effort, it established several new agencies, including the Central Council for Saving Promotion, the Savings Promotion Department of the Bank of Japan, and

---

7. "Employees Getting More: Investment Education, Planning Help on the Increase," *Pension & Investments*, January 23, 1995, p. 74.

the Savings Promotion Center of the Ministry of Finance. Promotional activities included monthly seminars extolling the virtues of saving and providing workers with financial guidance, sponsorship of children's banks, and appointing private citizens as savings promotion leaders. These agencies have also prepared and disseminated a variety of printed materials, advertisements, and films. The Japanese rate of saving rose precipitously over the relevant time period, but other factors were also at work, including strong tax incentives for saving, as well as various aspects of postwar reconstruction. One can therefore only speculate about the extent to which the increase in saving was attributable to promotion.

Several recent studies have begun to investigate the effects of retirement education in the workplace (Bernheim and Garrett 1996; Bayer, Bernheim, and Scholz 1996; Bernheim 1996c; Clark and Schieber 1996; and Yakoboski and VanDerhei 1996). These studies consistently find that workers significantly increase their saving once they are exposed to certain educational interventions. Programs with frequent seminars appear to be particularly effective.

In light of this evidence, it appears that the public sector could play an important role in promoting education and in establishing saving as a highly visible national priority. More immediately, it can promote financial education in the workplace by modifying and clarifying existing regulations to permit employers to undertake these activities without exposing themselves to unreasonable liabilities.

OTHER OPTIONS

From time to time, those who question the efficacy of tax incentives and other measures suggest that the government should simply adopt a program of mandatory saving (e.g., Gale and Litan 1993). Although this might sound draconian, there is ample precedent for forced saving in the United States. Social Security originated as a program of forced saving, and some proposals for privatization would reestablish this feature. A shortcoming of this approach is that it fails to distinguish between instances where individuals save too little to meet their own objectives and instances where low saving reflects the fully informed expression of personal preferences.

Aside from increasing the rate of saving, public policy can also address the saving gap by reducing the costs of retirement. The most straightforward way to accomplish this is to reduce the length of the retirement period. Significant increases in the average age of retirement would go a long way toward alleviating the personal and public financial imbalances that are expected to emerge in the next century. As David Wise points out in another chapter in this volume, increases in the normal age of retirement for Social Security are not likely to alter retirement patterns significantly. Such measures are, in effect, equivalent to benefit cuts; absent effects on retirement patterns, they simply widen the personal saving gap. A more promising strategy for increasing the average age of retirement is to raise the age of eligibility for early retirement under Social Security.

References

Arthur D. Little, Inc. *America's Retirement Crisis: The Search for Solutions.* Final Report to Oppenheimer Management Corporation, June 1993.

Attanasio, Orazio P. "Personal Saving in the US." Mimeo, Stanford University, February 1993.

Auerbach, Alan J., and Laurence J. Kotlikoff. *The United States' Fiscal and Saving Crises and Their Implications for the Baby Boom Generation.* Merrill Lynch, Pierce, Fenner & Smith, Inc., February 1994.

——. "U.S. Generational Accounts: An Update." Mimeo, Boston University, February 6, 1995.

Auerbach, Alan J., Laurence J. Kotlikoff, and David N. Weil. "The Increasing Annuitization of the Elderly—Estimates and Implications for Intergenerational Transfers, Inequality, and National Saving." Mimeo, University of Pennsylvania, 1992.

Avery, Robert B., and Michael S. Rendall. "Estimating the Size and Distribution of Baby Boomers' Prospective Inheritances." Mimeo, Cornell University, forthcoming.

Bayer, Patrick J., B. Douglas Bernheim, and J. Karl Scholz. "The Effects of Financial Education in the Workplace: Evidence from a Survey of Employers." Mimeo, Stanford University, 1996.

Berg, Olena. "DOL to Launch Savings and Pension Education Campaign." *EBRI Notes*, June 1995.

Bernheim, B. Douglas, "Dissaving after Retirement: Testing the Pure Life Cycle Hypothesis." In Z. Bodie, J. Shoven, and D. Wise, eds., *Issues in Pension Economics.* Chicago: NBER–University of Chicago Press, 1987.

———. *Is the Baby Boom Generation Preparing Adequately for Retirement? Summary Report.* Merrill Lynch, Pierce, Fenner & Smith, Inc., January 1993.

———. *The Merrill Lynch Baby Boom Retirement Index.* Merrill Lynch, Pierce, Fenner & Smith, Inc., July 1994.

———. "Do Households Appreciate Their Financial Vulnerabilities? An Analysis of Actions, Perceptions, and Public Policy." In Charles E. Wallar, Mark A. Bloomfield, and Margo Thorning, eds., *Tax Policy and Economic Growth.* Washington, D.C.: American Council for Capital Formation, 1995a.

———. "The Merrill Lynch Baby Boom Retirement Index: Update '95." Mimeo, Stanford University, 1995b.

———. "The Merrill Lynch Baby Boom Retirement Index: Update '96," Merrill Lynch & Co., Inc., 1996a.

———. "Rethinking Saving Incentives." In Alan Auerbach, ed., *Fiscal Policy: Lessons from Economic Research.* Cambridge, Mass.: MIT Press, 1996b.

———. "Financial Illiteracy, Ecucation, and Retirement Saving." In Olivia S. Mitchell and Sylvester J. Schieber, eds., *Living with Defined Contribution Plans.* Philadelphia: Pension Research Coucil, Wharton School of Management, 1996c.

Bernheim, B. Douglas, and Daniel M. Garrett. "The Determinants and Consequences of Financial Education in the Workplace: Evidence from a Survey of Households." Mimeo, Stanford University, 1996.

Bernheim, B. Douglas, Robert Lemke, and John Karl Scholz. "U.S. Household Saving in the 1980s: Evidence from the Surveys of Consumer Finance." Mimeo, Stanford University, 1997.

Bloom, David E., and Richard B. Freeman. "The Fall in Private Pension Coverage in the U.S." NBER working paper No. 3973, 1992.

Bosworth, Bary, Gary Burtless, and John Sabelhaus. "The Decline in Saving:

Evidence from Household Surveys." *Brookings Papers on Economic Activity*, 1991, p. 2.

Central Council for Savings Promotion. *Savings and Savings Promotion Movement in Japan*. Tokyo: Bank of Japan, 1981.

Congressional Budget Office (CBO). *Baby Boomers in Retirement: An Early Perspective*. Washington, D.C.: CBO, September 1993.

Clark, Robert, and Sylvester J. Schieber. "Factors Affecting Participation Rates and Contribution Levels in 401(k) Plans." In Olivia S. Mitchell and Sylvester J. Schieber, eds., *Living with Defined Contribution Plans*. Philadelphia: Pension Research Coucil, Wharton School of Management, 1996.

Cutler, David M., James M. Poterba, Louise M. Sheiner, and Lawrence H. Summers. "An Aging Society: Opportunity or Challenge?" *Brookings Papers on Economic Activity* 1 (1990): 1–56.

Diamond, Peter A. "A Framework for Social Security Analysis." *Journal of Public Economics* 8, no. 3 (December 1977): 275–98.

Engen, Eric, William G. Gale, and John Karl Scholz. "Effects of Tax-Based Saving Incentives on Saving and Wealth: A Review of the Literature." *Journal of Economic Perspectives*, November 1996.

Gale, William G., and Robert E. Litan. "Saving Our Way Out of the Deficit Dilemma." *Brookings Review*, fall 1993, pp. 6–11.

Hamermesh, Daniel S. "Consumption during Retirement: The Missing Link in the Life Cycle." *Review of Economics and Statistics* 66, no. 1 (February 1984): 1–7.

Hubbard, R. Glenn, and Jonathan S. Skinner. "The Effectiveness of Saving Incentives: A Review of the Evidence." *Journal of Economic Perspectives*, November 1996.

Hurd, Michael D. "The Adequacy of Retirement Resources and the Role of Pensions." Mimeo, State University of New York at Stony Brook, October 1993.

Kennickell, Arthur, and Janice Shack-Marquez. "Changes in Family Finances from 1983 to 1989: Evidence from the Survey of Consumer Finances." *1992 Federal Reserve Bulletin* 78 (1992): 1–18.

Kotlikoff, Laurence J. "Intergenerational Transfers and Saving." *Journal of Economic Perspectives* 2, no. 2 (spring 1988): 41–58.

Kotlikoff, Laurence, Avia Spivak, and Lawrence Summers. "The Adequacy of Savings." *American Economic Review* 72, no. 5 (December 1982): 1056–69.

Levin, Laurence. "Demand for Health Insurance and Precautionary Motives for Savings Among the Elderly." *Journal of Public Economics* 57, no. 3 (July 1995): 337–67.

Mankiw, N. Gregory, and David N. Weil. "The Baby Boom, the Baby Bust, and the Housing Market." *Regional Science and Urban Economics* 19 (May 1989): 235–58.

Modigliani, Franco. "The Role of Intergenerational Transfers and Life Cycle Saving in the Accumulation of Wealth." *Journal of Economic Perspectives* 2, no. 2 (spring 1988): 15–40.

Papke, Leslie E. "Are 401(k) Plans Replacing Other Employer-Provided Pensions? Evidence from Panel Data." NBER working paper No. 5736, August 1996.

Poterba, James M., Steven F. Venti, and David A. Wise. "How Retirement Saving Programs Increase Saving," *Journal of Economic Perspectives*, November 1996.

Reagan, Patricia B., and John A. Turner. "Did the Decline in Marginal Tax Rates during the 1980s Reduce Pension Coverage?" Mimeo, Ohio State University, June 1995.

Schieber, Sylvester J., and John B. Shoven. "The Consequences of Population Aging on Private Pension Fund Saving and Asset Markets." NBER working paper No. 4665, March 1994.

Sheiner, Louise, and David N. Weil. "The Housing Wealth of the Aged." NBER working paper No. 4115, 1992.

U.S. Department of Labor, Pension and Welfare Benefits Administration, Office of Research and Economic Development. "Private Pension Plan Bulletin: Abstract of 1992 Form 5500 Annual Reports," no. 5, winter 1996.

Vaupel, James W. "Uncertainties and New Evidence about the Prospects for Longer Life Expectancy." Mimeo, Odense University, Denmark, 1992.

Venti, Stephen F., and David A. Wise. "Aging, Moving, and Housing Wealth." In David A. Wise, ed., *The Economics of Aging*. Chicago: University of Chicago Press, 1989.

———. "But They Don't Want to Reduce Housing Equity." In *Issues in the Economics of Aging*. Chicago: University of Chicago Press, 1990.

Yaboboski, Paul, and Jack VanDerhei. "Pension Education: What Works?" In Olivia S. Mitchell and Sylvester J. Schieber, eds., *Living with Defined Contribution Plans*. Philadelphia: Pension Research Coucil, Wharton School of Management, 1996.

Keeping Savers from Saving

John Saver died at age seventy leaving an estate worth $1.9 million dollars; his wife had died two years earlier. He had saved conscientiously throughout his lifetime, hoping to have a long and comfortable retirement and believing that, were he to die prematurely, his children would benefit from his saving. Most of his saving was through a defined contribution pension plan to which he and his employer had contributed throughout his career. The contributions, which were placed each month in a stock fund, had accumulated to $1.2 million by the time of his death. Not knowing exactly what his firm plan would be worth, he had also saved through a personal individual retirement account (IRA) in which he had accumulated $100,000. He had a house and other assets worth $600,000. He was confident that, by consuming a bit less and saving a bit more while he was working, his children would be much better off than the children of his friend Jimmy

We are grateful to Henry Aaron, Joel Dickson, John Freidenrich, Steven Lockwood, Tom MaCurdy, Jim Poterba, and Seth Weingram for helpful comments and discussions. Jon Rork has provided superb research assistance. We acknowledge the financial support of the National Institute on Aging and the Hoover Institution (Wise), and Charles Schwab and BZW Barclays Global Investors (Shoven).

Spender, who had saved little. In 1982, John Saver would have been right. At that time his children would have been left with $60,000 of the last $100,000 that John had saved. But in 1996 he was wrong. His children were left with only $15,000 of this $100,000. Although John didn't know it—because he had worked until seventy and had not thought to check for hidden legislation—had he started to withdraw saving from his retirement plans at that age, he would have paid a marginal tax rate of 61.5 percent on his retirement income. What had happened in the meantime?

Over this period the introduction of personal retirement saving plans provided a large inducement to save through individual retirement accounts and 401(k) plans. Indeed, saving through these plans now far exceeds saving through traditional employer-provided defined benefit and defined contribution pension plans. A large body of evidence shows that contributions to these plans have worked to increase personal saving.[1] At the same time, however, and virtually hidden from the public eye, congressional legislators imposed harsh penalties on persons who unwittingly chose to save too much in retirement accounts. Whereas in 1982, pension assets were not subject to any estate taxes, by 1985 they were fully taxed as part of the estate. In addition, the excess distribution and excess accumulation taxes, the so-called success taxes, had been slipped into 1986 tax legislation. Possibly 80 percent of total personal saving is by way of employer or personal pension plans. Virtually all thoughtful observers believe that Americans save too little and that the low saving rate will limit prospects for future

---

1. For a detailed review of the evidence, see Poterba, Venti, and Wise (1996a). Poterba, Venti, and Wise (1996b) is a shorter and less technical review of the evidence. The evidence is also evaluated by Hubbard and Skinner (1996), who conclude that these programs have worked to increase saving. In his review of the evidence, Bernheim (1996) concludes that 401(k) plans have significantly stimulated personal saving, but he finds the IRA evidence harder to interpret, concluding that high estimates may be biased upward and low estimates biased downward A contrary view is argued by Engen, Gale, and Scholz (1996).

economic growth nationwide and at a personal level will endanger the economic well-being of future elderly Americans. Why then are the most consistent savers penalized for saving in the way that most saving is done?

In this chapter, we consider the evolution of the legislation that created virtually confiscatory tax rates on pension assets. Although we focus on the taxation of only one type of saving—albeit the singlemost important saving vehicle in the United States—we hope that the analysis and discussion will direct attention to laws that to us seem hard to justify. Perhaps our chapter may be thought of as a case study of tax legislation gone awry. We consider who might be affected by these tax rates now and who may be affected in the future. In the first section, we briefly review the new programs introduced in the early 1980s to increase saving and review the legislation that, when revealed and understood, will surely reduce saving. In the second section, we consider who might be affected by the excess distribution and excess accumulation taxes and conclude that these taxes are not limited to the wealthy. Indeed, consistent savers with modest earnings who invest prudently may be faced with these penalty taxes. Rather than just taxes on the rich, these are widespread penalties placed on lifetime savers. In the third section, we consider the saving of Americans now approaching retirement age and the potential saving of future generations of retired persons. Although most families who are on the eve of retirement now have saved very little, as personal saving plans spread a large proportion of lifetime savers could face excess distribution tax rates on retirement income withdrawn from these accounts, and many of these families would see their saving virtually confiscated if they died with substantial assets in retirement accounts. In the concluding section we summarize our findings and comment more generally on issues that the analysis raises.

Background

PROGRAMS TO ENCOURAGE SAVING

The two important saving programs introduced in the early 1980s were motivated by the low American saving rate, as well as the concern that many Americans reached retirement with little personal saving. Individual retirement accounts (IRAs) became available to all employees as part of the Economic Recovery Tax Act of 1981 and rapidly became a popular form of saving in the United States. Any employee could contribute $2,000 a year to an IRA account, and a nonworking spouse could contribute $250. The contribution was tax deductible. Annual contributions grew from about $5 billion in 1981 to about $38 billion in 1986, approximately 30 percent of total personal saving. The Tax Reform Act of 1986 limited the tax advantages of IRAs for higher-income persons, and contributions declined precipitously thereafter, even though the legislation limited the tax deductibility of contributions only for families who had annual incomes over $40,000 and who were covered by an employer-provided pension plan. By 1994, only $7.7 billion was contributed to IRAs. Whereas more than 15 percent of tax filers contributed in 1986, fewer than 4 percent contributed in 1994.

The other program introduced in the early 1980s was the 401(k) plan. Although formally created in 1978, 401(k)s were not used much until after 1981, when the Treasury Department issued clarifying regulations that made it possible for employers to establish these plans. Thereafter, 401(k) saving grew continuously and almost unnoticed, with contributions increasing from virtually zero at the beginning of the decade to more than $64 billion by 1992, when over 30 percent of families contributed to a 401(k). Contributions to 401(k) accounts are also tax deductible, and the return on the contributions accrues tax free; taxes are paid on withdrawal. But these plans are available only to employees of firms that offer such plans. Before 1987 the employee contribution limit was $30,000, but the Reform Act of 1986 reduced the limit to $7,000 and indexed this limit for inflation in subsequent years. The contribution limit was $9,235 in 1995.

By 1986, contributions to all personal retirement saving plans exceeded contributions to traditional employer-provided pension plans. Although contributions to IRAs declined precipitously after 1986, 401(k) contributions continued to grow, and now saving through these plans far exceeds saving through traditional employer-provided defined benefit plans, as shown in figure 1. In 1992, contributions to all personal retirement saving plans totaled $81 billion and contributions to traditional employer-provided defined benefit and defined contribution plans totaled $64 billion. It seems evident that, were it not for the Tax Reform Act of 1986, personal retirement plan saving would have been much larger.

Figure 1   Retirement Contributions

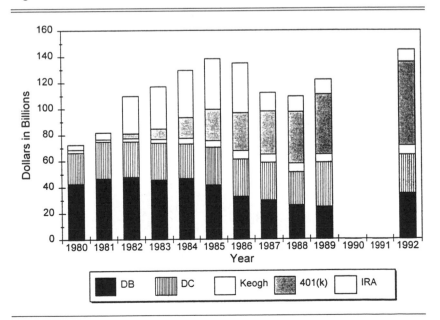

Saving for retirement through employer-provided and personal pension plans together now accounts for a large proportion of personal saving. Figure 2 shows both contributions to all retirement accounts and total personal saving as defined in the National Income and Product Accounts (NIPA). Over the past several years retirement saving has accounted for between 70 and 80 percent of personal saving. It seems apparent that major encouragement or limitation of this form of saving can easily have an important effect on national saving rates.

TAXES TO LIMIT SAVING

Hidden behind the success of IRA and 401(k) saving, however, is the danger that accumulated saving through these programs will be virtually confiscated at death and that a substantial fraction of withdrawals will be subject to a 15 percent surtax that can raise the tax rate on withdrawals to more than 60 percent. To understand how drastically

Figure 2   National Saving and Total Retirement Contributions

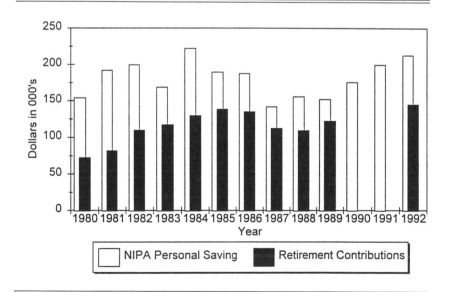

legislation has changed to create this situation, we begin by considering how the same estate would have been taxed in four different years: 1982, 1984, 1988, and 1996. In each of these years a person with an estate of $1.9 million dies at age seventy. Each estate is composed of $600,000 in nonpension assets including a house, $1.2 million in a defined contribution pension plan, and $100,000 in a supplemental IRA. Table 1 shows the tax rates on this estate in each year. The average combined estate and excise tax rate was seven times as high in 1996 as in 1982—29.16 percent versus 4.17 percent. What about the tax on the supplemental IRA plan? The marginal combined estate and excise tax rate on this plan, which was 0.00 percent in 1982, had been increased to 53.25 percent by 1996. The total marginal tax rate on the supplemental plan—including the estate tax, the excise tax, and state and federal income taxes paid by heirs—had risen from 39.23 percent in 1982 to 85.40 percent by 1996. Thus the heir in 1982 received more than $60,000 of the $100,000 IRA plan, whereas the heir in 1996 received less than $15,000.

Although startlingly high, the 1996 rates in this example are not atypical. We will describe cases in which the total marginal tax rate on pension plan assets in an estate ranges from 92.0 to 96.5 percent. The highest rate we have documented exceeds 99 percent. The changes between 1982 and 1996 evolved through several different legislative packages and affected several different taxes.

The estate tax on pension assets changed dramatically with the Tax Equity and Fiscal Responsibility Act of 1982, which became effective in 1983. Before this, pension assets—whether employer-provided defined benefit or defined contribution plans or personal plans such as IRAs and Keoghs—were not subject to estate taxes at all. Pension saving was taxed on a consumption basis; taxes were only imposed when the saving was spent, either by the saver or by the saver's heirs. Ironically, this example of a consumption tax, which many economists believe should be the basis for the entire tax system, was erased by the 1982 legislation. This legislation limited to $100,000 the pension assets

Table 1   Average and Marginal Tax Rates Faced on a $1.9 Million Estate (in 1996 dollars)

Date of Death	Average Combined Estate and Excise Tax Rate on Total Estate	Marginal Combined Estate and Excise Tax Rate on Supplemental IRA Plan Assets	Marginal Combined Estate, Excise, and Income Tax Rate on Supplemental IRA Plan Assets
1982	4.17%	0	39.23%
1984	28.31%	43.00%	69.75%
1988	22.62%	43.00%	69.75%
1996	29.16%	53.25%	85.40%

excluded from estate taxes. Even that limited exclusion was repealed in the Deficit Reduction Act of 1984. Thus the heirs in 1982 paid no estate taxes at all on pension assets; in 1984 all pension assets were subject to estate tax.

Marginal federal estate tax rates range from 37 percent to 55 percent, which is the applicable rate between $3 million and $10 million and above approximately $21 million. Between $10 and $21 million the rate is 60 percent because of the phaseout of the "benefit" of the graduated rates. The federal tax law allows a limited credit for state inheritance taxes. A state can thus levy inheritance taxes up to this limit without increasing total estate taxes. Many states impose inheritance taxes at exactly this limit; such state levies are known as "soak up" taxes. Thus, in the examples below, we assume that the combined federal plus state estate tax rate is equal to the federal rate.

The second important change was the imposition of the excess distribution and the excess accumulation taxes as part of the Tax Reform Act of 1986. The apparent purpose of these taxes was to penalize savers who used the favorable tax treatment of pensions to accumulate saving beyond what legislators assumed might be required for a comfortable retirement. Beginning in 1987, a 15 percent penalty tax (in addition to the income tax) was imposed on retirement plan withdrawals exceeding $150,000 a year. The $150,000 limit remained the same until 1996, when it was raised to $155,000. Now it is indexed to inflation and will be increased from time to time in minimum increments of $5,000. The 15 percent surtax is not deductible against either federal or state income taxes, so it simply adds fifteen points to a household's marginal income tax rate on pension withdrawals. It is often referred to as the "success tax" since, in addition to saving itself, it can be triggered by successful investment or a successful career.

A companion 15 percent excess accumulation tax was also incorporated in the tax reform of 1986. The excess accumulation tax imposed a penalty on the estates of savers who die with pension accumulations deemed excessive. Excessive accumulation in 1997 is defined to be the value of a single-life annuity paying $155,000 a year for someone the same age, and thus with the same life expectancy, as the deceased. Pension plan assets exceeding this amount are subject to the extra 15 percent penalty tax.[2] The excess accumulation tax can be deferred if assets are transferred to a surviving spouse, so it only affects single persons, widows, widowers, and married individuals who name a nonspouse as a beneficiary.

The third change was to federal income tax rates. In 1982, the top marginal tax rate was 50 percent. The Tax Reform Act of 1986 lowered the top federal income tax rate to 28 percent, effective in 1988. As late as 1992, the top effective rate was 31 percent. The 1993 Deficit Reduction Act increased this rate substantially. The highest effective rate is now about 44 percent. The highest tax bracket set in the 1993 Deficit Reduction Act was 39.6 percent. But itemized deductions and personal

---

2. The IRS provides guidelines on the permissible rate of interest to use in determining the value of a single-life annuity and also provides a table of life expectancies. "Allowable" and "excessive" accumulations depend on age: using the currently proscribed life expectancy tables and the permissible 8.2 percent interest rate gives the following limits: $1,243,612 at age sixty-five, $1,165,166 at age seventy, $955,358 at age seventy-five, and $794,158 at age eighty.

exemptions are phased out at higher income levels.[3] The elimination of itemized deductions alone raises the 39.6 percent bracket to about 41 percent. Together with the elimination of personal exemptions, the effective federal income marginal tax rate can be as high as 44 percent for a family of four. In addition, a 2.9 percent Medicare tax is imposed on all labor income, which for employed persons is shared evenly between the employer and the employee. Self-employed persons pay the entire 2.9 percent. Thus a self-employed person could face a tax rate on labor income of nearly 47 percent.

Another important feature of the federal tax system is the tax on capital gains. Although this tax does not apply to pension assets, it has an important effect on the return on nonpension assets and thus on the relative return on pension versus nonpension saving. Increases in the value of assets are not taxed until the gains are realized. Realized gains resulting from the sale of assets are taxed at ordinary income tax rates, with one important exception: the maximum marginal tax rate on capital gains is 28 percent. Finally, the "cost basis" for inherited assets is reset to the value of the assets at the time they are inherited. Thus the appreciation of these assets from the time of purchase until death is not taxed.

State income taxes are also an important determinant of the marginal tax rate on pension plan withdrawals. Several states have no income tax, but in forty-three states marginal rates range up to 12 percent. State income taxes are deductible from income in calculating federal taxes. In the examples in this chapter we typically use the top California marginal tax rate of 9.3 percent. For a person in the 39.6 percent federal tax bracket, the effective combined federal and state marginal rate is 46.41 percent, accounting for the partial phaseout of itemized deductions.

The combined effect of these taxes is staggering. For example, a

---

3. Beginning at $117,950 for single tax filers and at $176,950 for married couples filing joint returns.

person in California who has saved too much for retirement and is thus subject to the excess distribution tax will face a marginal tax rate of about 61.5 percent, counting the federal income tax, the state income tax, and the penalty success tax. The combined marginal tax rate on estates is much more complicated but can be explained with the aid of table 2.

We assume that marginal inherited wealth (W) is subject to the 15 percent excess accumulation tax and that the combined federal plus state estate tax rate is 55 percent. The heir is subject to a 9.3 percent state income tax and a 41 percent federal income tax rate. In this case, 61.75 percent of the marginal estate goes to pay the excess accumulation and the estate tax. State income taxes, through a rather complicated formula, take an additional 8.54 percent. Finally, federal income taxes take 21.67 percent. Altogether, a whopping 91.97 percent of the marginal estate dollar goes to pay taxes.

Table 2   Illustration of Marginal Tax on Inherited Pension Wealth

Tax	*Paid On*	*Illustrative Tax*
Excess accumulation	Pension wealth W T_XW	.15W
Estate tax (federal and state)	Pension wealth less excess accumulation tax $T_E(1-T_X)W$	$.55(1-.15)W = .4675W$
Subtotal		$[.15+.55(1-.15)]W = .6175W$
State income tax	Pension wealth less state estate tax, which is paid on pension wealth less excess accumulation tax $\Pi = T_Y^s[1-(1-T_X)T_E^s]W$	$.093[1-(1-.15).096]W$ $= .093[.9184]W$ $= .0854W$
Federal income tax	Pension wealth less federal part of estate tax, which is paid on pension wealth less excess accumulation tax, less state income tax $T_Y^f[1-(1-T_X)T_E^f-\Pi]$	$.41[1-(1-.15).454-.0854]W$ $= .41[1-.4713]W$ $= .41[.5287]W = .2167W$
TOTAL TAX ON ESTATE		.9197W

A striking feature of this tax structure is that income taxes are paid on a large portion of the pension wealth that has already been used to pay the excess accumulation and the estate taxes. State income taxes are paid on 91.84 percent of pension wealth, even though only 38.25 percent of the estate remains after paying the excess accumulation and estate taxes; federal income taxes are paid on 52.87 percent of pension wealth. The illustrative rate shown here is far from extreme. The rate would be several points higher if the estate were in the 60 percent estate tax bracket. In addition, the rate would be even higher in New York or any other state where state estate taxes exceed the amount that the federal government allows as a credit against the federal estate tax. We have encountered rates as high as 99.73 percent.

Now retirees face a temporary reprieve from one of the penalty taxes. The recent legislation that raised the minimum wage was accompanied by the Small Business Protection Act of 1996, which temporarily suspended the 15 percent penalty tax on excess distributions. The penalty tax was apparently imposed in part to reduce short-run tax losses on pension plan contributions. Now the tax has been set aside in the hope that short-run tax revenues will increase. Ironically, the legislation suspended a tax that few people knew existed. Perhaps its elimination will increase awareness of it, which indeed is likely to reduce saving in the long term.

There is also a provision in the minimum wage legislation removing the requirement that withdrawals from pensions plans begin at age seventy and six months. Under the tax treatment of plan withdrawals and inheritances, however, delaying withdrawal may simply make the saver and his children worse off. A person who worked until death would receive no benefit from prior saving, and his children could receive only a small fraction of what he had saved.

One other legislative package also imposed important limits on saving, although not a tax on pension saving. The Omnibus Budget Reconciliation Act of 1993 reduced from $235,840 to $150,000 the maximum salary that can be used as a basis for contributions to employer-provided defined contribution plans. For example, before this legislation the contribution could have been 3 percent of $235,840; at the same rate, the legislation limited the contribution to 3 percent of $150,000. In addition, the legislation reduced from $235,840 to $150,000 the projected pension benefit that could be funded under a defined benefit pension plan. The limits are now $155,000, and both are indexed for inflation but only in $10,000 increments. Because pension plan contributions are such a large fraction of personal saving, it can be expected that this legislation will work to reduce saving.

Who Is Affected?

SAVERS

How rich do you have to be? How lucky? As it turns out, not very rich and not very lucky. Consider two people who begin work today and have these earnings and saving patterns:

	Person 1 *Schoolteacher*	Person 2 *MBA*
Start work at age	twenty-five	twenty-five
Initial salary	$25,000	$50,000
Real annual salary increases	2 percent	2 percent
Salary at age fifty	$41,015	$82,030
Pension contribution rate	10 percent	10 percent
Pension assets invested in	Growth stocks	S&P 500
Real rate of return	10 percent	8 percent

Both begin work at age twenty-five, receive real salary increases of 2 percent a year, and contribute 10 percent of their earnings to a defined contribution pension plan. Person 1, perhaps a schoolteacher, starts working at an annual salary of $25,000 and invests her pension assets in growth stocks with a real rate of return of 10 percent. Person 2, perhaps an MBA, earns $50,000 on her first job and invests her pension contributions in the Standard and Poor's 500 earning a real 8 percent a year. (Ibbotson Associates [1996]) reports that since 1926 the mean real rate of return on the S&P 500 has been 9.2 percent and the mean real rate of return on small company stocks has been 14.1 percent.)

The pension assets of the schoolteacher and the MBA at selected ages are shown in figure 3, together with the pension accumulation that would trigger the excess accumulation and distribution penalty taxes. (If, in the event of death, the estate would be subject to the excess accumulation tax, then distributions would typically be subject to the excess distribution tax if individual longevity were equal to life expectancy.) The MBA would have to pay the penalty tax if she retired at age sixty-two or older, the schoolteacher if she retired at sixty-four or older. Demographic forces are likely to lead to increases in the typical retirement age in the coming decades, as discussed by Wise (1996). If the schoolteacher and the MBA should choose to work until age seventy, both would have pension assets far above the level that would trigger the penalty taxes.

Real historical data on rates of return can be used to illustrate the situation of a hypothetical software engineer who entered the labor force in 1971 at age twenty-five. We consider the same person but assume different investment choices:

	Person 3 Software Engineer		
Pension investment in	*Stocks*	*Corp. Bonds*	*Half and Half*
Starts work in 1971 at age	twenty-five	twenty-five	twenty-five
Initial salary	$15,000	$15,000	$15,000
Real annual salary increases			
Until age fifty	2.5 percent	2.5 percent	2.5 percent
After age fifty	1.0 percent	1.0 percent	1.0 percent
Salary in 1996 at age fifty	$102,500	$102,500	$102,500
Pension contribution rate	10 percent	10 percent	10 percent
Rate of return 1971–95	Actual	Actual	Actual
Rate of return thereafter	8 percent	4 percent	8 percent and 4 percent

Figure 3   Pension Accumulation, Schoolteacher and MBA

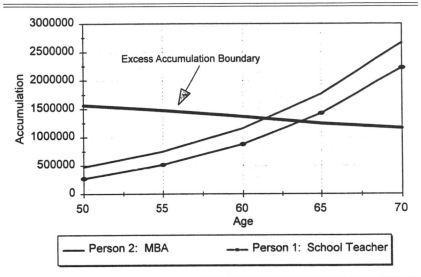

The pension asset accumulations at selected ages under these three investment choices are shown in figure 4, together with the pension accumulation that would trigger the excess accumulation penalty tax. No matter what the investment choice, the software engineer would face the penalty tax were he to work until age seventy. If the engineer had invested in stocks, by age seventy he would accumulate pension assets more than three times as large as the allowable accumulation. To avoid the penalty tax, the engineer who invested in stocks would have to retire by age fifty-eight.

WHEN A SHELTER? WHEN A TRAP?

Whether it pays to save through a pension plan depends on the retirement income that could be supported through wealth accumulated in this way compared with the retirement income that would be provided by "conventional" saving—outside a pension plan. We consider the annuity that would be provided at retirement age if saving

John B. Shoven and David A. Wise

Figure 4   Pension Accumulation, Software Engineer

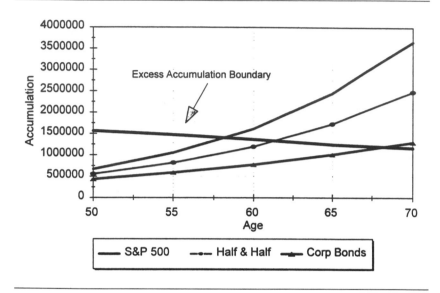

were in a pension compared with the annuity that could be provided through conventional savings. This comparison depends on whether the prospective saver will face the excess distribution tax when withdrawals are made from the pension fund in retirement. But the annuity that the accumulated wealth will support also depends on the tax treatment of the return on saving. The return on all saving in a pension fund is taxed the same; when funds are withdrawn they are taxed at the ordinary personal income tax rate (plus the excess distribution penalty if applicable). But the return on conventional saving depends on how the saving is done. If investment is in bonds, the comparison is simple: the return on corporate bonds held outside the pension system is taxed at the personal income tax rate. The return on municipal bonds held outside a pension is not taxed at all. With stock investments the comparison is more complicated: dividends are taxed at the personal income tax rate, realized capital gains are taxed at the capital gains rate, and unrealized capital gains are not taxed (until realized).

We consider a marginal increase in saving. The question is whether the saving should be done through a pension plan or through conventional means. To provide illustrative comparisons we consider a person who will

Begin work at age thirty

Receive nominal annual wage increases of 6 percent

Retire at age seventy

Make equal pension withdrawals between seventy and eighty-five

Face combined federal and state marginal tax on labor income of 46.41 percent

Face a capital gains tax of 28 percent

Receive a nominal return on bonds of 8 percent

Receive a nominal return on stocks of 11 percent

Based on formulas described in detail in Shoven and Wise (1996), we calculate the ratio of the retirement annuity that could be supported through extra pension saving versus the annuity that would be supported through extra conventional saving. In making the calculations, we ensure that before-tax pension contributions and after-tax conventional saving leave the person with the same consumption out of income before retirement. The results under alternative circumstances are presented in table 3. The first alternatives pertain to bond investments and the subsequent ones to stock investments.

A person investing in corporate bonds who will not face the penalty tax will do much better saving through a pension plan. Pension saving yields 2.68 times as much in retirement income as conventional saving, as shown for case 1 in the table. This is undoubtedly the situation that financial advisers foresee when they advocate saving through pension plans, often suggesting pension contributions up to the limit that the law allows. But the advantage is not always so great. A savvy person who realized that the best outside alternative would be in municipal rather than corporate bonds would gain only 33 percent by investing through

Table 3   Advantage of Marginal Pension
          Saving Under Selected Circumstances

Circumstance	Ratio of Retirement Annuity: Pension to Conventional Saving
Invests in bonds (8% return):	
1 Begins saving at age 30 Without penalty: tax on pension withdrawals 46.41% Conventional saving alternative is corporate bonds	2.680
2 Begins saving at age 30 With penalty: tax on pension withdrawals 61.41% Conventional saving alternative is municipal bonds	1.330
3 Begins saving at age 40 With penalty: tax on pension withdrawals 61.41% Conventional saving alternative is municipal bonds	1.176
4 Begins saving at age 40 36% instead of 39.6% federal income tax bracket With penalty: tax on pension withdrawals 58.6% Conventional saving alternative is municipal bonds	1.096
Invests in stocks (11% return):	
5 Begins saving at age 30 2% of return in dividends 2% of return in realized capital gains 7% of return in unrealized capital gains Without penalty: tax on pension withdrawals 46.41%	2.012
6 Begins saving at age 30 2% of return in dividends 2% of return in realized capital gains 7% of return in unrealized capital gains With penalty: tax on pension withdrawals 61.41%	1.449
7 Begins saving at age 30 11% of return in unrealized capital gains With penalty: tax on pension withdrawals 61.41%	0.956
8 Begins saving at age 30 11% of return in unrealized capital gains 36% instead of 39.6% federal income tax bracket With penalty: tax on pension withdrawals 58.6%	0.891

a pension plan, as shown for case 2. A person whose outside investment would be in municipal bonds, who would face the excess distribution tax on pension fund withdrawals, and who doesn't start to save until age forty would gain less than 18 percent (case 3). The municipal bond investor who would face the penalty tax and who will be in the 36.0 percent instead of the 39.6 percent federal income tax bracket would gain less than 10 percent from the pension saving option.

For a stock investor, the comparison is somewhat more compli-cated because the outside return depends on how the return is re-ceived. Case 5 assumes that 2 percent of the 11 percent nominal return is in dividends, 2 percent is in realized capital gains, and 7 percent is in unrealized capital gains. If the person will not face the penalty tax, pension saving yields about twice as much in retirement income as conventional saving. If the person will face the penalty excess distribu-tion tax, the advantage of pension saving is less than 45 percent (case 6). If the person will face the penalty tax and the alternative to pension saving is outside investment in stocks (or a stock fund), which generates only unrealized capital gains, the pension alternative is a net loser, as shown under case 7 in the table. In this case, pension saving yields less than 96 percent of the retirement income that would be provided through conventional saving. If, in addition to the case 7 circum-stances, the person were in the 36.0 instead of the 39.6 percent federal income tax bracket, at the time of retirement the pension saver would have almost 11 percent less in retirement income.

Instead of considering a higher pension contribution rate over a career, one can consider a onetime contribution to a pension plan with a known future withdrawal date. As above, the question is whether to save in a pension or through conventional means. Again a distinction must be made between bond and stock investments. In either case, if the tax rate on pension fund withdrawals is less than the income tax rate, it always pays to save through a pension. If this is not the case, as when the excess distribution tax is imposed, then the important consid-eration is how long the money must be invested for the higher tax-deferred return under the pension plan to offset the penalty tax on withdrawal of pension assets at retirement. It all depends. But for bond investments, a typical break-even holding period might be around fifteen years. For shorter periods, conventional saving dominates pension saving. For stock investments the holding period can be anywhere from about ten years to forever, depending on how the return is paid outside the pension plan. If all return is in the form of unrealized capital gains, the pension will never pay. If 2 percent is in dividends, 2 percent in realized capital gains, and 7 percent in unrealized capital gains, a typical holding period would be about eleven years.

The illustrations above make clear that a pension is not always the best way to save for retirement. Indeed, if additional retirement saving will trigger the excess distribution tax, the added retirement income provided by additional pension plan saving may be less than the income that would be provided through conventional saving. But income in retirement is only part of the story. Many savers will die with assets still in pension plans. What will the heirs receive from additional saving that passes through an estate? We consider a person who saves an additional dollar that will be invested for thirty years. The accumulated assets will then pass through an estate and will be subject to the excess accumulation tax. What proportion of the additional saving will end up in the hands of the children? The answer depends on the investment return, the total value of the estate, and the estate and income tax rates faced by the heirs. We assume these conditions: the assets will accumulate for thirty years, the bond nominal rate of return is 8 percent, and the nominal rate of return on stocks is 11 percent.

Maintaining these assumptions, we consider several cases that are described in table 4. In each case, the table shows these three values: the tax rate on the incremental saving done through a pension plan, the ratio of the net amount received by the children under pension saving versus the amount received under conventional saving, and the break-even holding period for both forms of saving to yield the same net bequest to the children. The total marginal tax rate on the estate is

Table 4	Net Income to Heirs from Supplemental Saving That Passes through an Estate

Circumstance	Total Marginal Tax Rate on Estate (in %)	Loss from Pension Saving (in %)	Break-even Years
Bond investment			
Total value of estate $3.1 million Heir is in the 39.6% federal income tax bracket	91.97	35	49
Total value of estate $1.6 million Heir is in the 36% federal income tax bracket	83.86	0	30
Total value of estate $10.1 million Heir is in the 39.6% federal income tax bracket	96.41	67	80
Stock saving			
Total value of estate $3.1 million Heir is in the 39.6% federal income tax bracket 2% dividends, 2% cap gain, 7% unrealized cap gain	91.97	48	74
Total value of estate $3.1 million Heir is in the 39.6% federal income tax bracket 11% unrealized capital gains	91.97	67	never
Total value of estate $1.6 million Heir is in the 36% federal income tax bracket 2% dividends, 2% cap gain, 7% unrealized cap gain	83.86	20	45
Total value of estate $1.6 million Heir is in the 36% federal income tax bracket 11% unrealized capital gains	83.86	49	never
Total value of estate $10.1 million Heir is in the 39.6% federal income tax bracket 2% dividends, 2% cap gain, 7% unrealized cap gain	96.41	74	120
Total value of estate $10.1 million Heir is in the 39.6% federal income tax bracket 11% unrealized capital gains	96.41	83	never

calculated following the rather tortuous rules described in table 2 above.

The total marginal tax on the estate depends only on the total value of the estate: on an estate of $3.1 million the tax is 91.97 percent; it is 83.86 percent on an estate of $1.6 million and a whopping 96.41 percent on an estate of $10.1 million. In all cases, save one, the net amount passed to the children is much larger under conventional than pension saving. The break-even period is at least forty-five years except in one case. With one exception, the loss from pension saving after thirty years ranges from 20 percent to 83 percent of the amount that would go to the heirs if the saving had been done outside the pension system. In short, pension saving that is subject to the excess accumulation tax is essentially confiscated if it passes through an estate. The children of these savers would receive much more if additional saving were done outside the pension system.

The confiscatory tax rates give a large incentive to savers for taking money out of pension plans (see Shoven and Wise 1996). Thus the taxation of pensions not only discourages additional saving but also encourages some savers to withdraw funds in retirement even if the funds are not wanted for consumption. Funds that would otherwise be left in the pool of saving available to finance economic investment may be used for current consumption simply to avoid confiscation by the tax collectors.

Who Could Be Affected?

Perhaps several million taxpayers will pay excess distribution and accumulation taxes in the near future. Still, only a small proportion of all persons now nearing retirement have accumulated enough pension saving to trigger the excess distribution and accumulation taxes. Indeed, measured by the median, the typical family on the eve of retirement (with a head aged fifty-one to sixty-one) has only $40,000 in retirement assets, including the value of employer-provided pensions and personal retirement accounts. The median of nonretirement financial assets is a paltry $7,000. But with the expansion of 401(k) plans in particular, a much larger proportion of future retirees is likely to be victimized by these taxes.

Data from the Health and Retirement Survey (HRS) on the financial assets of families with heads between fifty-one and sixty-one in 1992 are reported in table 5 by income percentile. The percentile interval is shown in the first column, and the corresponding income range within each interval, in the second column. Median financial assets are shown in columns 3 through 5 and means in columns 6 through 8. Retirement asset levels—including employer-provided pensions as well as IRA, 401(k), and Keogh plans but excluding Social Security—are shown in columns 5 and 8. Nonretirement financial assets are shown in columns 4 and 7. Total financial assets—the sum of the previous two categories—are shown in columns 3 and 6. Two facts are clear from these data: most families on the eve of retirement have accumulated very little in nonretirement financial assets, and retirement assets are modest. Typically a large fraction of what has been accumulated is retirement saving. For example, families with incomes between the 80th and 90th percentiles have median financial assets of $173,165. The median of retirement assets is $123,383 and the median of nonretirement assets is $23,000. Overall, retirement saving accounts for almost 71 percent of total financial asset saving.

These data indicate that about 55 percent of financial assets are owned by families in the top 30 percent of the income distribution, as shown in column 9 of table 5. Families with income below the 30th percentile own only about 15 percent of the total. The top 30 percent of families account for about 55 percent of retirement saving; the bottom 30 percent of wage earners account for only about 14 percent of retirement saving. Thus, if saving incentives are to generate more

Table 5   Median and Mean Financial Assets of Health and Retirement Survey Respondents by Income Percentile, 1992

		MEDIANS ($1,000s)			MEANS ($1,000s)			PERCENT OF TOTAL	
Income percentile interval	Annual income interval ($1,000s)	All financial assets	Non-retirement financial assets	Retirement assets: employer, IRA, 401(k) & Keogh	All financial assets	Non-retirement financial assets	Retirement assets: employer, IRA, 401(k) & Keogh	All financial assets	Retirement assets
(1)	(2)	(3)	(4)	(5)	(6)	(7)	(8)	(9)	(10)
<10	<$7.9	10.5	0.5	0.0	94.6	42.5	52.1	0.06	0.04
10–20	$7.9–$14.4	9.8	1.0	1.2	75.5	26.6	48.9	0.04	0.04
20–30	$14.4–$20.0	23.8	1.8	10.2	76.3	19.7	56.7	0.05	0.05
30–40	$20.0–$26.0	41.5	4.0	20.0	100.3	39.0	61.3	0.06	0.05
40–50	$26.0–$33.0	58.4	7.2	40.0	113.0	36.6	76.4	0.07	0.07
50–60	$33.0–$40.1	82.0	8.0	59.8	139.8	35.1	104.6	0.08	0.09
60–70	$40.1–$49.0	106.1	10.0	74.1	164.5	45.4	119.1	0.10	0.10
70–80	$49.0–$60.0	146.8	20.0	87.5	210.8	57.7	153.1	0.13	0.13
80–90	$60.0–$79.0	173.2	23.0	123.4	255.9	75.1	180.8	0.15	0.15
90–100	>$79.0	322.0	50.0	229.2	452.8	138.8	314.0	0.27	0.27
90–95	$79–$101	301.2	34.5	203.7	369.7	96.2	273.5	0.11	0.12
95–100	>$101	380.0	74.0	256.6	542.8	185.0	357.8	0.16	0.15
98–99	$135–$187	391.2	103.0	232.0	486.7	184.3	302.4	0.03	0.03
99–100	>$187	543.0	150.7	340.5	883.7	350.9	532.7	0.05	0.05

NOTE: These calculations are based on all HRS families with wage income in 1992.

saving they must almost by definition induce persons with higher incomes to save more, for it is likely that the bulk of the increase will necessarily come from higher-income families.

These data make clear that there is substantial room for greater saving at higher-income levels, as well as at lower levels. To give some idea of the assets that would be accumulated with persistent saving over a working career, we have roughly approximated the assets that the HRS families would have accumulated had they saved consistently for retirement throughout their lives. We proceeded this way: (1) We identified the income decile of each family in the 1992 wave of the HRS. (2) For the years 1957 to 1992, we calculated household earned-income percentiles by age, and for each income percentile we calculated median family income. Estimates for 1964 to 1992 are based on the annual March Current Population Surveys (CPSs). Estimates for earlier years are based on the 1964 CPS and estimates and changes in median earned income for the entire population. (3) Then we constructed a lifetime earnings profile for each HRS family by assuming that a family in a given income percentile in 1992 was a member of the same decile in all years since age twenty-five. (4) We assumed that nominal earnings of the household will grow at 4 percent between 1992 and the year that the household head reaches age sixty-five. (5) Finally, we calculated nominal accumulated saving through age sixty-five and converted the nominal amount to 1993 dollars using a 3 percent discount rate. The results for saving rates of 10 percent and 15 percent and for nominal investment returns of 6.0 percent and 12.2 percent (the mean annual returns on bonds and stocks—the S&P 500—between 1926 and 1995) are shown in table 6.

In all income intervals, saving at these rates would have led to financial asset accumulation much larger than actual accumulations. For example, if the families with earnings between the 80th and 90th percentiles had always earned at that level, had saved 10 percent of pretax income, and had earned a return of 12.2 percent, accumulated financial assets at sixty-five would be $1,139,000. If the saving rate had

Table 6   Median Estimated Financial Assets of Health and Retirement
Survey Respondents if Had Specified Lifetime Saving,
by Income Percentile

Income Percentile Interval	Income Interval ($1,000s)	ASSETS AT 65 IF HAD SAVED FROM 25 TO 65 ($1,000S)			
		Save 10% earn 6%	Save 10% earn 12.2%	Save 15% earn 6%	Save 15% earn 12.2%
(1)	(2)	(9)	(10)	(11)	(12)
<10	<$7.9	24	103	36	155
10–20	$7.9–$14.4	65	272	98	408
20–30	$14.4–$20.0	96	393	144	590
30–40	$20.0–$26.0	124	498	185	747
40–50	$26.0–$33.0	152	599	228	899
50–60	$33.0–$40.1	184	716	276	1074
60–70	$40.1–$49.0	217	831	326	1246
70–80	$49.0–$60.0	256	961	385	1442
80–90	$60.0–$79.0	310	1139	465	1708
90–100	>$79.0	440	1547	661	2321
90–95	$79–$101	440	1547	661	2321
95–100	>$101	440	1547	661	2321
98–99	$135–$187	454	1596	680	2394
99–100	>$187	440	1547	661	2321

been 15 percent and the return 12.2 percent, the accumulation at sixty-five would be $1,708,000. The actual median of HRS families in these earnings percentiles is only $173,165. The average age of the HRS respondents is only fifty-six, however, so current assets could easily more than double by age sixty-five. Nonetheless, these potential saving accumulations are in stark contrast with the actual saving of these families; with the illustrative lifetime saving rates and investment returns, even families with the lowest earnings would have accumulated sizable wealth at retirement age. For example, families in the lowest 10 percent of earnings would have accumulated $155,000 if they had saved 15 percent and had a nominal investment return of 12.2 percent.

At a saving rate of 10 percent and a return of 12.2 percent, these households would have accumulated $103,000.

Even with widespread participation in 401(k) plans, the saving rates evaluated in the simulations may be high and the rates of return too optimistic. Nonetheless, it is easy to see that consistent lifetime saving, perhaps through a 401(k) plan, would yield large asset accumulations for a substantial fraction of households. Referring back to figures 3 and 4, which show the accumulated pension assets that would trigger the excess distribution and accumulations taxes, it is clear that many millions of future consistent savers should anticipate such taxes.

Finally, we have tried to give some idea of the number of current HRS households who could face the excess accumulation tax by the time they retire. To do this, we have assumed that, *including additional contributions*, pension assets will grow at 10 percent until retirement. If all HRS respondents retired at sixty-five, approximately 6 percent would have pension assets exceeding the penalty threshold. If they all worked until age seventy, perhaps 16 percent would face the penalty tax. This means that, over the whole population, around one million households could face the excess distribution tax if they worked until sixty-five and perhaps three million could face the tax if they worked until age seventy. Although only a small proportion of all household heads will work past age sixty-five, a larger proportion of wealthier households will retire after age sixty-five.

In summary, we are concerned in this chapter with the implications of the tax treatment of retirement saving. Although these data suggest that only a small fraction of persons have to date accumulated large retirement assets, the accumulation of future savers is likely to be larger than the current levels. Indeed, the 401(k) program is still growing, and any further expansion of this program could have a substantial effect on the saving of future generations of elderly households. Thus if the inducements to save through 401(k) and other personal retirement plans were successful (and there is substantial evidence that more and more employees are participating in such plans), a large fraction of families could accumulate substantial assets. A large portion of these families would face the "success" tax, and for many only a tiny fraction of retirement assets left as a bequest would end up in the hands of their heirs.

Conclusions and Discussion

Since the early 1980s the introduction of the IRA and 401(k) programs has worked to increase individual saving. Now more saving is done through these plans than through conventional employer-provided defined benefit and defined contribution plans. Altogether, pension plan saving for retirement accounts for at least 70 percent of personal saving. Although encouraging saving with one hand, however, legislators have worked with the other, a mostly hidden hand, to discourage the very retirement saving that accounts for the bulk of personal saving in the United States. In 1982, pension saving was not subject to estate taxes and was taxed only when the funds were withdrawn either by the pension saver in retirement or by the saver's children. This consumption tax treatment is the scheme that many economists believe yields the greatest economic growth and that was a key feature of each of the major tax reform proposals discussed in the past two years. Yet in 1997 pension saving that passes through an estate can be virtually confiscated through a series of estate, income, and "excess accumulation" penalty taxes imposed on large accumulations of pension saving, and large withdrawals from pension plans are subject to an "excess distribution" penalty tax. We find

- That the marginal tax rate on large distributions is likely to be as high as 61.5 percent and that the confiscatory marginal tax rates on large pension assets passing through an estate can be as high as 92 percent to 97 percent and sometimes even higher.

- That these extraordinary tax rates are not limited to the rich. Rather, they are taxes on lifetime savers. For example, a person with median earnings over a long career who contributes 10 percent of earnings to a 401(k) plan with assets invested in the S&P 500 is likely to be victimized by these "success" taxes. Although only a small proportion of persons now approaching retirement will pay these taxes, the rapid expansion of 401(k) plans in particular will place a large number of future savers in harm's way.

- Many lifetime savers will find that the prospect of these taxes completely offsets the incentive to save for retirement in a pension plan. The prospect that most of the funds will be confiscated if pension assets remain at death provides an enormous incentive to limit pension saving. Furthermore, these taxes provide a large incentive to withdraw saving from pension funds before it is needed for consumption. All work to limit the saving of those who would otherwise save the most.

Savers who increase their saving because of the opportunities offered through personal or employer pension plans do not reduce resources available to the rest of the population. Indeed, the gain to savers from consuming tomorrow rather than today is only a portion of the social return from the increment to the pool of saving. Assuming that increased saving leads to increased investment and thus economic growth and, indeed, more taxes in the future, the social return far exceeds the private gain.

Then what lies behind policies to keep savers from saving? A complete accounting is not possible here. But at least three forces have lurked behind the scenes of saving legislation. One is the widely held view that saving leads to economic growth and will improve the lot of future elderly; combined with the equally widespread belief that the saving rate in the United States today is too low, this view suggests that saving should be encouraged. This was an important motivation for the Economic Recovery Tax Act of 1981, which made IRAs available to all employees, and for the 1978 legislation that established the foundation for 401(k) plans. A second force has been the desire to curb the chronic federal budget deficit, which has led to curtailment of the very saving plans that were intended to encourage saving. This force gives great weight to the short run and little weight to the long-run growth of the economy. The tendency has been to avoid short-run tax expenditures at the expense of long-run revenues. A third force, and perhaps the most troubling, is the view that saving incentives such as those provided through IRA and 401(k) plans are a gift to the wealthy and thus that their use should be limited for that reason. From this perspective comes the notion that too much saving in this form should be penalized. It ignores the social gain from saving no matter what the mechanism that induces it. All three forces have been at work over the past decade and a half.

It has always been true that most saving is done by people with the most money. That is still the case. If saving is to be increased, people with the greatest income must be induced to save more of it. Since many families with high incomes have accumulated little wealth on the eve of retirement, it is hoped that the inducement to save will add to the financial security of future retirees, even those with higher lifetime incomes. Although Americans of all income levels could benefit by saving more, the bulk of any increase is likely to come from persons with the highest incomes. Encouraging them to save while penalizing them for taking advantage of the inducement is likely to curtail economic growth. An inducement to save, although viewed by some as a gift to the rich, might more properly be viewed as a way to get the rich to use more of their resources to contribute to the national well-being. The United States will benefit more if a wealthy person saves a million dollars than if the wealthy person uses the million to buy a bigger house.

If economic growth is to be quickened and if the well-being of future elderly is to be enhanced, the relative power of the three forces will have to change. The United States can only be hurt by keeping savers from saving.

References

Bernheim, Douglas. 1996. "Rethinking Saving Incentives." Unpublished manuscript, Stanford University.

Engen, Eric, William Gale, and John Karl Scholz. 1996. "Effects of Tax-Based Saving Incentives on Saving and Wealth: A Review of the Literature." *Journal of Economic Perspectives*. November.

Hubbard, R. Glenn, and Jonathan S. Skinner. 1996. "The Effectiveness of Saving Incentives: A Review of the Evidence." *Journal of Economic Perspectives*. November.

Ibbotson Associates. 1996. *Stocks Bonds, Bills, and Inflation: 1996 Yearbook*. Chicago: Ibbotson Associates.

Poterba, James, Steven Venti, and David Wise. 1996a. "Personal Retirement Saving Programs and Asset Accumulation: Reconciling the Evidence." NBER working paper #5599.

———. 1996b. "How Retirement Saving Programs Increase Saving." *Journal of Economic Perspectives* 10, no. 4 (fall).

Shoven, John, and David Wise. 1996. "The Taxation of Pensions: A Shelter Can Become a Trap." NBER working paper #5815. November.

Wise, David A. 1996. "Retirement against the Demographic Trend: More Older People Living Longer, Working Less, and Saving Less." NBER working paper. Forthcoming in *Demography*.

Medical Care Reform
for an Aging Society

It is many years in the future. After decades of rapid cost increases, Medicare has become the largest government program, with only Medicaid approaching that amount. The spending has taken its toll; the trustees of the Medicare Trust Fund report that the trust fund has only three months left before insolvency. Political panic ensues. Everyone agrees that something must be done but not what that should be. A proposal is made to cut Medicare payments to physicians, but the American Medical Association announces that it will urge doctors to boycott nonemergency Medicare patients if this occurs. An alternative proposal is made to increase the costs of Medicare to seniors, but the American Association of Retired Persons says that it will vigorously oppose this option. A third proposal is made to increase payroll taxes to pay for Medicare, but this too is a nonstarter. A rich billionaire offers to take over management of the current Medicare system for only 95 percent of current payment amounts, but fears of the elderly suffering at the hands of a for-profit entrepreneur doom this proposal.

After three months of debate, no option garners majority support. The political system is deadlocked. Finally, Medicare cannot pay its bills. Medicare payments are by law reduced 30 percent, so that the system does not go bankrupt.

Marketplace havoc erupts. Doctors and hospitals decide to violate Medicare payment rules and bill patients privately for the amount above the Medicare payment. Companies that issued supplemental insurance poli-

cies, held by more than half the elderly, refuse to cover these additional payments. As a result, out-of-pocket payments for the elderly rise. In turn, more elderly are pushed into providers of last resort—charity clinics and doctors that take care of the poor. But the strain is too great. The fountain of private insurance payments that kept charity care alive refuses to support the elderly in need. Charity providers announce they will restrict their "free care" to the nonelderly only.

Many seniors, unable to afford the required additional payments, go without care. Horror stories appear. An elderly woman, without the means to supplement the Medicare amount, sits in an emergency room for two days while the hospital tries to find a charity provider for her. An elderly man dies in an ambulance because no hospital would accept the patient without knowing his financial status. Common conditions such as arthritis and lacerations go untreated.

After two months of confusion, a deal is struck. The elderly will pay more for Medicare. Payroll taxes will be increased. Providers will accept lower payments. The Medicare Trust Fund is "saved"—at least for another fifteen years.

A fanciful scenario? Perhaps. But in the 1996 election both "tax increases" and "cutting Medicare" were dirty words, despite the fact that the Medicare Hospital Insurance Trust Fund is projected to go bankrupt in 2001 and that health care is consuming the federal budget. Our current path will result in the scenario above by the dawn of the next century.

We are headed for a crisis over how much medical care society can afford and who will pay for that care. Unlike Social Security, we don't have the luxury of years in which refined debate can narrow down disparate options. Whether we want to or not, we need to make fundamental decisions about the nature of our medical guarantee, and we need to make those decisions soon. In this chapter, I talk about the issues we face and the options on the table.

There is no shortage of difficult issues plaguing the medical sector. Fifteen percent of Americans are uninsured, creating concern that society is not meeting its obligations to the less fortunate. Even for people with insurance, coverage is often fleeting; people are insured when they are healthy but may be dropped or face premium increases if they become sick. That too is a public concern.

But far and away the dominant health care issue facing the country is the cost of medical care. The United States spends nearly 14 percent of national income—close to one in every seven dollars—on medical care. Nearly 20 percent of government spending is for medical care. Virtually every medical care problem we face—from caring for the uninsured to cherry picking by insurers—is made worse when medical costs are high. The place to start in understanding our medical system is with the cost of that system, which is what I address in this chapter.

Projecting Medical Care Costs

How large a problem will medical care be for society over the next several decades? Two issues stand out in forecasting medical spending: the aging of the population and the intrinsic growth of medical costs.

AN AGING SOCIETY

Older people, naturally, use more medical care than do younger people. In 1987 people under nineteen used $745 per person of medical services compared with $1,500 for prime-age adults, $3,700 for the young elderly (ages sixty-five to sixty-nine), and more than $9,000 for the oldest elderly (ages eighty-five plus) (see figure 1).

Given this great disparity in medical care spending by age and the fact that the U.S. population will age rapidly over the next several decades, forecasts are for a substantial increase in medical spending over time. Between 1990 and 2010, aging will not have a great effect on medical spending; per capita medical spending will increase by only 3 percent (see table 1). Between 2010 and 2050, however,

Figure 1   Medical Care Spending by Age

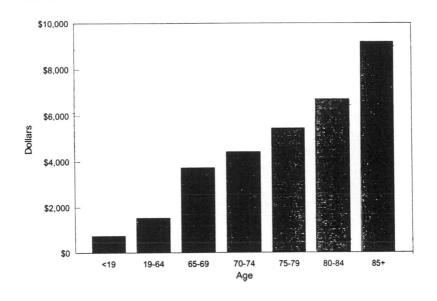

SOURCE: Department of Health and Human Services

population aging will increase spending on medical care by nearly one-quarter.

Of course, population aging will affect a wide variety of public and private institutions, including Social Security, private pension plans, housing markets, and stock markets. But the effect is likely to be greater for medical care than for these other institutions because medical spending is concentrated at upper ages. Average Social Security payments are roughly the same at different ages. Thus, expected Social Security payments depend almost entirely on the total number of elderly, not the composition of the aged population. Medical spending, in contrast, increases substantially with age, even within the elderly population (see figure 1). Thus, shifts in the age distribution *within* the elderly population will also affect medical care spending. Indeed, the

David M. Cutler

Table 1   Projections of Medical Spending

Year	AGING		INTRINSIC GROWTH	
	Per capita spending	*Index (1987=1)*	*Per capita spending*	*Index (1987=1)*
1987	$1,766	1.00	$1,766	1.00
2010	1,825	1.03	2,625	1.49
2030	2,079	1.18	3,900	2.21
2050	2,297	1.30	5,796	3.28

NOTE: Spending is in real (1987) dollars. Population projections are from the Bureau of the Census. Health spending is from the Department of Health and Human Services.

most rapidly growing part of the elderly population is projected to be the group over age eighty-five—where medical spending is the highest. The increase in medical spending is therefore magnified relative to the increase in Social Security spending or spending by private pensions.

No one disputes the fact that aging will increase medical spending, but some uncertainties exist about the magnitude of this effect. The first is demographic. Forecasting the number of oldest elderly (aged eighty-five plus) is particularly perilous since it depends a great deal on medical advances in the treatment of cancer and heart disease and other factors such as diet and exercise that we have little ability to forecast. It is generally thought that the Census Bureau projections (which underlie table 1) understate the degree to which the very aged population will increase. Thus, table 1 may *understate* the forecast of increases in medical spending.

In addition, age-specific medical spending may change over time. We typically relate health spending to age, but this is not the right underlying model. A more appropriate model relates health spending to *disability*, which increases with age but may also change over time. Indeed, evidence suggests that disability rates have been falling in recent years (Manton 1996). Thus, age-specific medical spending is likely to fall, suggesting that the estimates above may be too high.

We do not know the importance of each of these two factors over the next half century. But, as a benchmark, an estimate of a 30 percent increase in medical spending resulting from population aging seems appropriate.

THE GROWTH OF MEDICAL COSTS

Beyond aging, there is an additional issue in the medical care context that has enormous implications for society—the fact that per person spending on medical care is increasing rapidly. For people of a given age, medical spending has increased dramatically over time (see table 2). Over the ten-year period between 1977 and 1987 medical spending rose in each age group, by 25 to 50 percent in real terms.

This ten-year period was not unusual, nor is this growth particular to the United States. Table 3 shows medical spending in the Organization for Economic Cooperation and Development (OECD) as a whole in 1960 and 1990. Although the data are not adjusted for demographic changes, such changes over the 1960–1990 period were small compared with projected changes in the next century. Between 1960 and 1990, real per capita medical spending in the United States increased by 4.7 percent annually, nearly twice the growth rate of real gross domestic product (GDP). Similar trends are true for the Group of Seven countries and the OECD as a whole. The average country now spends nearly 8 percent of GDP on medical care, with a high of

Table 2   Medical Spending by Age

	PER CAPITA SPENDING		
Age	1977	1987	*Increase*
Total	$1,234	$1,776	44%
<19	505	745	48
19–64	1,221	1,535	26
65+	3,481	5,360	54

NOTE: Spending is in 1987 dollars.
SOURCE: Department of Health and Human Services.

David M. Cutler

Table 3   Trends in Per Capita Medical Spending and Income

Country	MEDICAL SPENDING ($1990)			Real Gross Domestic Product (GDP) Growth	Medical Spending/ GDP, 1990
	1990	1990	Growth		
Canada	$473	$1,770	4.4%	1.8%	9.5%
France	326	1,532	5.2	2.4	8.8
Germany	425	1,486	4.2	1.8	8.3
Italy	223	1,236	5.7	2.5	8.1
Japan	117	1,171	7.7	2.7	6.7
United Kingdom	349	972	3.4	1.5	6.2
United States	621	2,566	4.7	2.8	12.2
G-7 average	$407	$1,808	5.0%	2.1%	8.5%
OECD average*	$376	$1,680	5.0%	2.2%	8.0%

* The Organization for Economic Cooperation and Development (OECD) average excludes Luxembourg, Portugal, and Turkey, because the data were not available in 1960.
SOURCE: OECD.

more than 12 percent in the United States. Throughout the developed world, increases in medical spending are putting increasing strains on social resources.

To get some sense of what this implies, table 1 shows projections of per capita medical spending over the next half century if medical costs increase by 2 percent a year.[1] If this growth rate occurs, medical care costs will increase by more than 50 percent in the next twenty years, and by 230 percent by the middle of the next century.

IMPLICATIONS

Both population aging and the underlying growth of medical costs will raise medical spending over time. To account for the magnitude of these two effects, the upper line in figure 2 shows projections for the

---

1. This is roughly the growth rate of medical spending above the growth of the economy as a whole; thus it is the increasing burden of medical care over time, which is analogous to the increasing burden from aging.

Figure 2   Health Expenditures as a Share of Gross Domestic Product

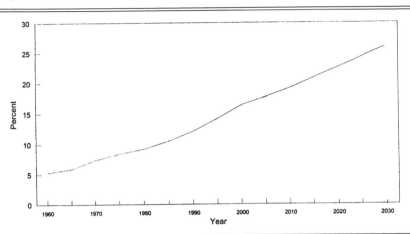

SOURCE: Department of Health and Human Services

share of GDP devoted to medical spending between now and 2030. By 2030, health spending will reach more than 25 percent of GDP and will continue to increase beyond 2030.

In large part this burden will be borne by the public sector. Nearly two-thirds of medical spending for the elderly is financed publicly, compared with only one-quarter of spending for the nonelderly (see table 4). Thus, spending increases will particularly affect the public sector.

Public spending on medical care is predominantly from two sources.[2] Medicare is the largest government health program, spending about $5,000 per beneficiary. Ninety percent of Medicare beneficiaries are elderly; the remaining 10 percent are disabled or receiving end-stage renal disease treatment. Medicaid is a large and increasing part of medical care. Medicaid provides care for poor women and children (one-third of total spending), the disabled (one-third), and the elderly (one-third). Importantly for the aging society, Medicaid covers nearly

---

2. See Cutler (1996) for an overview of the public-sector involvement in medical care.

David M. Cutler

Table 4   Use of Medical Services by Age

	AGE		
	<19	*19–64*	*65+*
Total	$745	$1,535	$5,360
Percent public	27%	26%	63%
Percent private	73%	74%	37%

SOURCE: Health Care Financing Administration.
NOTE: Acute services are hospital and physician care.

half of long-term care expenses for the elderly. More than one-third of medical spending for the population aged eighty-five and over is nursing home expense. As this population increases, the burden on Medicaid will rise.

To get a sense of the impact of these trends on the public sector, the lower line in figure 2 projects the share of GDP devoted to Medicare (no similar projections are made for Medicaid). Where Medicare in 1997 is less than 3 percent of GDP, by 2030 it will be nearly 8 percent. Note that federal spending as a whole accounts for only about one-fifth of GDP, so this represents an increase of nearly 25 percent of the current federal obligation.

Of course, the revenues for this spending must come from somewhere. Currently, public-sector medical spending is financed in two ways. Part A of Medicare, which covers inpatient services, is paid by a trust fund (the Hospital Insurance Trust Fund), which collects revenues from a 2.9 percent payroll tax. Part B of Medicare, which covers outpatient services, and all of Medicaid are financed through general revenues.

Because there is a trust fund for Part A services, there is a separate accounting for the costs of those services. To illustrate the magnitude of the medical care problem for the public sector, figure 3 shows projections of the assets of the Hospital Insurance Trust Fund over the next decade. The Hospital Insurance Trust Fund has close to $130

Figure 3   Assets of the Hospital Insurance Trust Fund

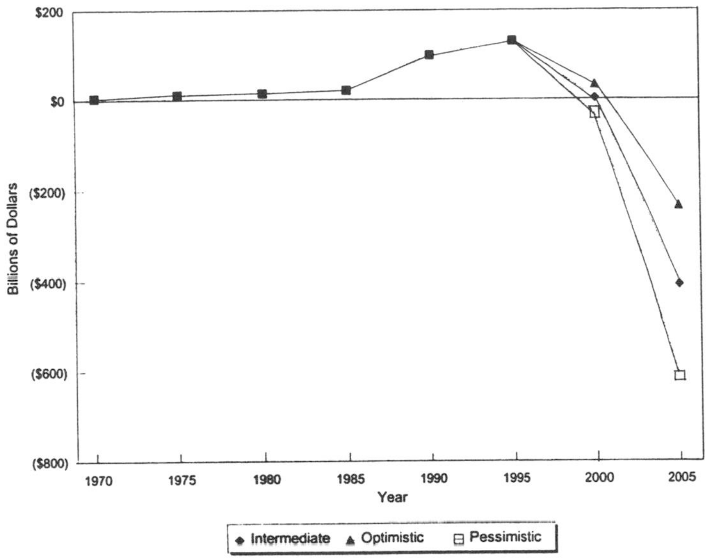

SOURCE: HI Trust Fund

billion in assets now, but those assets will not last. Current projections indicate that the trust fund will go bankrupt early in the next century. In the benchmark case, insolvency occurs in 2001, and by 2005 the trust fund is projected to run a $400 billion deficit. Even under the optimistic scenario, insolvency is projected in 2001, and the trust fund will have a deficit of $234 billion in 2005. This is the scare scenario with which I began the chapter.

Of course, from an economic perspective, it means little to talk about the solvency of one part of the government. If the government wanted to extend the Hospital Insurance Trust Fund, it need only move services from Part A to Part B or use general revenues to supplement the payroll tax. Only the government budget as a whole really matters in determining public-sector solvency, and the government as a whole is far more solvent than the Hospital Insurance Trust Fund.

But consideration of the trust fund illustrates the magnitude of the medical care problem facing society, which is a useful purpose. And it serves another purpose as well; since entitlement programs are not reauthorized every year, they do not change except in rare circumstances. Politically, it is always easier to let a popular program continue as it is than to consider reforms that would hurt some people. The impending insolvency of the Hospital Insurance Trust Fund forces the Medicare issue onto the table in a way that would not otherwise occur.

In addition to their implications for the public sector, rising health costs will also affect private incomes. As table 4 shows, private spending on medical care is nearly $2,000 annually among the elderly, $1,000 for prime-age adults, and $500 for children. As medical care costs increase, these out-of-pocket payments will increase as well. Ensuring an equitable burden of out-of-pocket payments is a major concern for society.

To put it another way, under current projections medical care will account for one-quarter of GDP by the middle of the next century. *Someone* must pay that bill. We may choose indirect sources of financing—for example, through the government and thus taxes or through employers and thus lower wages—but we cannot escape the overall burden. The financing of a good that costs 25 percent of the average family's pretax income is a major public policy problem. We need to deal with it as such.

More fundamentally, if we want to reduce the overall burden of medical spending, we need to focus on reforms that lower overall medical costs, not just redistribute costs to different people. This is an important distinction to make in the discussion of medical care reform.

Why Medical Costs Increase

Before considering options for reducing medical spending, it is important to understand why medical costs are increasing so rapidly. Policy options will be very different if the reason for rising costs is higher profits of providers versus the provision of valuable services.

An accounting identity is helpful: spending on medical care is the sum of the prices paid for care and the amount of care received:

$$Spending = \sum_i P_i \cdot q_i$$

where P and q are prices and quantities for service i. Increases in spending on medical care can result from increased prices paid for services or increases in the number of services received. Empirical research is virtually uniform in the conclusion that *the dominant factor in the growth of medical care costs over time is the increasing quantity of services provided, not the price of given services.*

Let us consider the treatment of heart attacks.[3] Heart attacks are common (about 230,000 new cases in the Medicare population annually),[4] they are expensive but not unusually technologically intensive, and their acute nature makes it easy to measure changes in treatment. Medicare is a major payer for heart attacks. Indeed, if we add up hospital costs only in the year following a new heart attack, Medicare spent $2.6 billion on heart attacks in 1984 (adjusted to 1991 dollars) and $3.4 billion in 1991,[5] for an annual growth rate of 3.9 percent (see the first row of table 5).

What accounts for this nearly 4 percent annual growth in spending on heart attacks? One potential explanation is an increase in the number of people with heart attacks. In fact, however, the number of new heart attacks was essentially constant from 1984 to 1991 (see the second row of table 5). In contrast, spending per heart attack, shown in the

---

3. The example is taken from Cutler and McClellan (1996).

4. These figures exclude the elderly enrolled in managed care. This is a growing but small share of the elderly population.

5. Total Medicare spending on inpatient care was $63 billion in 1991.

David M. Cutler

Table 5   Accounting for the Growth of Spending on Heart Attacks, 1984–1991

AMI Treatment	INTENSIVE PROCEDURE USE			AVERAGE REIMBURSEMENT		
	1984	1991	Annual change*	1984	1991	Annual change
Total Spending ($bn)				$2.6	$3.4	3.9%
Number of Patients				233,295	227,182	−0.4
Average Spending				$11,175	$14,772	4.0%
Type of Treatment						
Medical management	88.7%	59.4%	−4.2%	$9,829	$10,783	1.3%
Catheterization only**	5.5	15.5	1.4	15,380	13,716	−1.6
Angioplasty	0.9	12.0	1.6	25,841	17,040	−5.9
Bypass surgery	4.9	13.0	1.2	28,135	32,117	1.9

NOTE: Reimbursement for 1984 is in 1991 dollars, adjusted using the GDP deflator. Price and quantity indexes use 1991 weights.

* Growth is average percentage point change each year.

** Patients who received catheterization but no revascularization procedure. Patients who received bypass surgery or angioplasty will also have had a catheterization.

SOURCE: Cutler and McClellan (1996).

third row of the table, increased by 4.0 percent annually between 1984 and 1991.

To understand what is responsible for cost growth, it helps to know more about the treatment of a heart attack. The least invasive treatment is medical management, which typically involves drug therapy, monitoring, and counseling and treatment for reducing risk factors such as high cholesterol levels and smoking. There are important choices here—such as whether to use a drug to dissolve the clot and which drug to use—but this branch does not involve major surgical procedures.

An alternative to medical management is one or more invasive cardiac procedures. Invasive treatment begins with a *cardiac catheterization*, a diagnostic procedure that documents areas of no or limited blood flow that may be involved in the current or possible subsequent heart attacks. If the catheterization detects important blockages in the arteries supplying the heart, more-intensive *revascularization* procedures may be used to treat the blockages: coronary artery bypass surgery (CABG), a highly intensive, open-heart surgical procedure to bypass occluded regions of the heart's blood flow, or percutaneous transluminal coronary angioplasty (PTCA), a procedure whereby a balloon-tipped catheter is inserted into the blocked artery and inflated with the goal of restoring blood flow.

Naturally, Medicare pays much more for patients receiving intensive surgery than for patients not receiving intensive surgery. In 1991, bypass surgery was reimbursed at three times the rate of medical management and angioplasty was reimbursed 60 percent more than medical management (see table 5). But these payments have not increased substantially over time. Payments for angioplasty, for example, fell as Medicare officials realized it was reimbursed too highly in 1984 relative to its true severity. Prices for the other services changed little in real terms.

In contrast, procedure use has increased substantially. In 1984, 11 percent of patients received a catheterization, with 5 percent of patients going on to receive bypass surgery and 1 percent receiving angioplasty (see table 5). By 1991, 41 percent of patients had received a catheterization, with 13 percent also receiving bypass surgery and 12 percent also receiving angioplasty.

How much of the rise in costs is because of this explosion in the use of high-tech procedures and how much is due to price changes? Essentially all the increase in spending is a result of increases in the quantity of intensive treatments provided (see table 6). Price changes have had essentially no effect on increases in total spending.

Whether this conclusion generalizes to other diseases is, of course, uncertain. But an emerging consensus is that the spread of medical technology explains most of the long-run growth in medical costs (Aaron 1991; Fuchs 1996; Newhouse 1992; Weisbrod 1991).

David M. Cutler

Table 6   Accounting for the Growth of Heart Attack Spending

Component	*Share*
Total	100%
Quantity increase	76%
Price increase	−6
Covariance	31

SOURCE: Cutler and McClellan (1996).

SHOULD WE CARE ABOUT RISING HEALTH COSTS?

Since increased medical spending results primarily from aging and increased service use, one might argue that there is no need to worry about spending on medical care. After all, spending increases on medical care (or any good) are valuable if they are buying services worth more than they cost.

This is an important issue. Unfortunately, there are no systematic data on the value of medical services that can be used to answer this question. From the data that are available, I suspect we will reach two conclusions. On the one hand, we are likely to find that the *average* value of medical care is high. If we look at medical care over the past thirty years, for example, the changes in medical practice that we have observed for the average patient are most likely associated with improvements in health outcomes worth far more than their cost. Indeed, Cutler, McClellan, Newhouse, and Remler (1996) estimate that, in the heart attack example discussed above, the average patient lived an additional eight months in 1991 beyond what he lived in 1984. If a life year is valued at $25,000, the additional life span is well worth the cost.

On the other hand, we are almost certain to find that the *marginal* value of that technology—the value to the last recipient—is low. There is ample evidence for this view. The Rand Health Insurance Experiment (Manning et al. 1987; Newhouse et al. 1993), for example, found that people who were better insured used more medical care than those who had less generous insurance but that their health outcomes were no better. Other research shows that differences in the use of medical care in different areas of the country (Wennberg et al. 1987), in different hospitals (Staiger and Gaumer 1990; Cutler 1995), or over time (Garber, Fuchs, and Silverman 1984; Kahn et al. 1991; Cutler and Staiger 1996) frequently keeps people alive for several months but not as long as a year. A number of studies have looked at the value of medical care directly, concluding that the value of high-tech medical care to marginal patients is low (Chassin et al. 1987; Winslow et al. 1988a, 1988b; Greenspan et al. 1988; McClellan and Newhouse 1995).

This finding is not surprising in light of the incentives built into the medical care system. Traditionally, patients paid little for medical care at the time they received services, and doctors were paid on a fee-for-service basis, giving them additional income for providing additional care. The result was incentives to provide care with any value, even if that value was low.

In addition to the insurance system, information problems mean that patients cannot always tell what services they should receive. In such a circumstance, people will frequently make poor choices about what is best for them. Finally, in the medical care case, unlike in many other goods, highly valued outcomes (such as survival) are at stake. As the probability of death increases, people are willing to spend essentially all the resources they control on medical care, even if the value of that care is low. This too leads to an overprovision of medical services from society's perspective.

Reforms that limited the amount of low-valued medical care could be of great value to society. My guess is that at least 15 percent of medical care currently provided has less value than it costs to provide. Eliminating this care would free up about 2 percent of GDP—a large amount.

In addition, a more rational health care system might have a different underlying growth rate of medical care costs. The factors noted above also create incentives for developing high-tech, high-cost medical care and minimizing the value of cost-saving technologies. A new technology that offers marginal improvements in health but has high cost, for example, will be demanded widely if patients see little explicit cost for its use. A new technology that offers slightly worse care but at substantially lower cost will not be in heavy demand if patients do not receive the cost savings. This "dynamic moral hazard" may explain why technology in medicine is almost uniformly associated with cost increases.

Options for Reform

I now turn to the question of what we should do about medical care costs. I group the potential solutions into three categories.

COST SHIFTING

The first solution is to reallocate costs in the health system. The idea behind this is straightforward: our current set of payments arose in a haphazard way. Since medical care is such a large burden for society, and will become an increasingly large burden as the population ages, we ought to reorient these payments.

In particular, the public sector is paying for an enormous share of medical expenditures for the elderly. In a period where the deficit has become an increasing concern, and where the real incomes of the elderly have increased, it is natural that the elderly should pay more of these costs themselves.

Increasing the costs of medical care to the elderly can be accomplished in several ways: increasing the premium charged for Medicare above the current 25 percent; increasing out-of-pocket cost sharing in

Medicare;[6] or raising the age of eligibility for Medicare. These changes could apply to all the elderly, to the high-income elderly, or to the elderly differentiated along some other margin, such as those with children capable of paying for their medical care or those with insurance to supplement Medicare.

Increasing the costs to the elderly for medical services is appealing. The bargain that was made with the elderly decades ago was agreed to when the elderly were the poorest members of society; today they are not. In addition, we did not know how much medical care would cost over time. Now that medical care has turned out to be expensive, that deal no longer seems fair. In addition to its redistributional implications, cost shifting may have valuable resource implications. If we increase the age of Medicare eligibility, for example, people may work to a later age, contributing more to Social Security and Medicare and adding to national output.

But cost shifting does not fundamentally affect the overall level of medical costs. Money that the government saves is money that the elderly must pay. Cost shifting does not reduce the overall resources of the medical system, nor does it make the medical care marketplace more efficient. Because these other issues are important, I do not believe we can make cost shifting the only component of our attempts to deal with the medical care issue.

PAYMENT REDUCTIONS

The second solution to rising health costs is to pay less for medical care. This seems noneconomic, but in fact has a sound economic logic. Many medical payments are a return on past investment. Doc-

---

6. I include this as a cost-shifting proposal rather than a spending reduction proposal since many of the elderly already have private insurance (Medigap) to cover their out-of-pocket costs, and thus increasing cost sharing will primarily increase Medigap premiums without affecting the costs paid at the margin.

tors, for example, are paid substantially above the cost of the services they provide because of expertise they acquired in the past. Put another way, the average cost of medical services provided is above their marginal cost.

In such a situation, payment reductions are an attractive way to reduce overall spending. Indeed, this is the method that many insurers have taken to limit spending on medical care. Health maintenance organizations (HMOs), for example, generally pay much less for the same services than do more generous insurance policies (Cutler, McClellan, and Newhouse 1997). Governments have traditionally limited spending on Medicare and Medicaid by reducing provider payments. Prices paid by Medicare, for example, have grown less rapidly than general inflation for most of the last decade.

Payment reductions are a natural way to limit spending in the short run. Given the services that are currently available, the easiest way to spend less is to pay less for what we are already receiving. That is why payment reductions are attractive when the goal is near-term deficit reduction—the traditional driver for public policy reforms in health care.

But the essence of the medical cost problem is a long-term problem, not a short-term one. Almost by definition, payment reductions cannot be a long-term solution. Consider the heart attack example noted above. For insurers to offset increases in spending on heart attacks by reducing the prices they pay for heart attack treatments, they would have to reduce real prices by roughly 3 percent a year, which can be done for only so long. Prices will fall below marginal cost, and providers will be unwilling to treat heart attack patients.

Payment reductions are particularly hard to sustain if they apply to only some patients. For example, if Medicare reduces payments for Medicare beneficiaries and private insurers do not follow, providers would be less willing to see Medicare patients and would substitute more privately insured patients. The converse is true as well. Indeed, this is what happened in Medicaid in the mid-1980s, when payments were reduced sufficiently far that access to appropriate care was a concern in many states.

Payment reductions thus cannot be a source of long-term cost savings in medical care. In acknowledging this, we implicitly rule out the source of most of the savings that the public sector (and the private sector) have realized in recent years. This is unfortunate.

SERVICE REDUCTIONS

Ultimately, if we want to spend less on medical care, we must receive fewer services. The question is, how can this be accomplished? The most attractive option is to start with the insurance system. One reason people choose to consume too much medical care is because they do not face the cost of that care when they decide what to receive. If we want people to make more appropriate choices about their use of medical resources, we should give them financial incentives to do so.

Traditionally, this policy option has led people to focus on increasing the amount people pay for medical care *when they are sick*. For example, there have been proposals to income relate Medicare cost sharing or to require high-deductible medical savings account (MSA) insurance policies that leave people exposed to more of the marginal costs of medical care.

These proposals strike me as unwise. If people want a policy more generous than an MSA, shouldn't they be allowed to purchase one? Requiring people to pay more at the time they receive medical care asks them to make an important financial decision when they are under strain, have little direct knowledge of the options involved, and have little time to do the necessary research.

A more natural alternative is to focus on the situation where people have the time and the ability to make better-informed choices—*when they purchase their insurance policy*. If people share in the costs of more generous insurance and receive the benefits of less generous insurance, there will be incentives to design better insurance policies—ones that provide only care that is worth more than its cost. In this view, it does not matter if people choose a policy with little cost sharing, provided people are willing to pay the additional costs of the insurance premium required for the policy. A system that relies on individual choice to decide on medical care services is often termed a "choice-based" insurance system (Cutler 1995, 1996; Aaron and Reischauer 1996).

To understand this system, think about it in its purest case. In a pure choice-based system, insurers would offer people a range of plans, differing in the degree of management, the amount of cost sharing, the services covered, and the price. People would pay more for a more-generous plan and receive the savings for a less-generous plan. Individuals would choose plans from a menu provided by the government or their employer.

In the Medicare program, establishing a choice-based system would amount to converting the current payment into a coupon amount and disbursing it to individuals. In the private sector, some employers—generally firms with many workers—already offer something close to this. Small firms, however, typically offer only one insurance policy, in large part because the administrative costs of offering multiple plans are high. Thus, one would need to encourage (or require) small firms to enter pools in which many insurance policies would be offered. In addition, current tax rules subsidize the purchase of more generous insurance by excluding employer payments and employee payments made with "cafeteria" plans from taxation. Thus, one would need to eliminate the tax subsidy to insurance, at least at the margin.

In theory, implementing insurance choice is simple. But, in practice, a workable choice-based system is difficult to achieve, and several issues would need to be addressed.

OVERSIGHT

Making effective choices requires having the knowledge to do so. Health insurance is a complex product, and people don't know the implications of all its provisions. Even if coverage is promised, it doesn't necessarily mean that the care is actually available if insurers have discretion in how services are provided. Thus, the government would have to regulate service provision and require that quality information be provided to consumers. This regulatory and informational role is common in many markets.

INSURER REGULATION

It is not enough to offer people choices in insurance; someone must be willing to sell to them at a price society thinks is appropriate. This is a particular concern in health insurance markets because insurers often know about people's health status before they enroll. Thus, if allowed to, insurers will charge sick people a high rate and healthy people a low rate to account for the differences in expected cost.

Allowing insurers to charge people more when they get sick is not true insurance, however; it just delays their medical care payment. Just as people want to be able to rely on being insured for medical care during a year, they also want to be insured against premiums increasing if they happen to get sick. Markets where insurance premiums vary with health status do not provide this insurance. Thus, a choice-based system must require that all people be charged the same amount or that premiums vary only along certain dimensions, such as age, sex, and location.

Even this does not solve the regulatory problem, however. If insurers charge everyone the same rate but have discretion in who they insure, they will choose to insure the healthy and turn away the sick. Thus, in addition to regulating premiums, the government also needs to regulate access to insurance and the right of renewal.

ADJUSTING PREMIUM PAYMENTS

Beyond these formal selection issues, there is an additional sorting issue. People's tastes for insurance policies are correlated with their health status. Sick people want few restrictions on their choice of providers; healthy people are more willing to bear such restrictions. In a choice-based system, even if everyone has access to the same insurance plans, healthy people will disproportionately enroll in some plans and sick people will disproportionately enroll in others. Premiums will reflect these differences; more generous plans will charge substantially more than less generous plans, in part because the people in these plans are less healthy.

Although plans offering more generous benefits should cost more if their services are better or they are less efficient, the fact that premiums are higher because people in these plans are sick is not beneficial. It penalizes the less healthy simply because they are less healthy. It also discourages the healthy from joining these plans since they would face above-average premiums to subsidize the less healthy. And it provides incentives for plans to encourage the less healthy not to enroll, so that they can attract healthier people.

This set of issues is empirically important. Consider the example of benefit changes at Harvard University, described in Cutler and Remler (1996). For many years, Harvard offered a generous insurance policy and a number of less-generous policies. Harvard subsidized the generous policy to keep it affordable. In 1995, in an effort to save money and promote competition, Harvard changed to an equal contribution rule—payments were equalized across plans. This increased the out-of-pocket price to enroll in the generous policy substantially. As expected, people left the generous plan. But the important fact was that the people who disenrolled were the relatively healthy group in the generous plan. As a result of this adverse selection, the generous plan lost a substantial amount of money and thus had to raise its premium in the second year. This, in turn, encouraged further disenrollment, again by the relatively healthy subscribers in the plan. By the end of the second year after the pricing change, it was clear that the generous plan could not survive under an equal contribution rule and the plan folded.

The Harvard system had some good points—overall premium growth slowed and the university saved money. But not setting prices well led to a number of problems, including the elimination of the market for more generous insurance.

If some mechanism is not found to correct for the health-based sorting of people, choice-based insurance will not work well. A natural solution is to pay more to plans that enroll a less healthy mix of people and less to plans that enroll a more healthy mix. Plans that are compensated for less-healthy enrollees will find that they can care for them without having to charge more to everyone else. Designing an appropriate set of adjusted payments will take time since the government needs to know which dimensions people sort themselves along and how well plans can identify these differences.

WILL CHOICE-BASED INSURANCE WORK?

A choice-based system will be difficult to implement, and regulation—to limit the practices of insurers, guarantee that services that are promised are actually delivered, and reduce the importance of nonrandom enrollment—must be part of it. And even regulation may not make the system work perfectly.

But my sense is that a choice-based system is the only option that may help reduce medical care costs in the long run. If we want to spend less on medical care, we need to limit the services that are provided. Allowing choices among insurance policies seems like the natural way to do this.

Conclusions

Health care reform encompasses many difficult aspects of public policy. Because the problem is most acute in the future, there is a temptation to delay reform. The losers are well identified whereas the winners are dispersed; thus there is a strong constituency against change. And health care is something we would like people to have more of, not less.

For those reasons, we may well find ourselves in the tragic scenario envisioned at the start. But important problems can bring valuable solutions. If we undertake meaningful reform now, the benefits could accrue to generations of people.

I want to conclude on one cautionary note. I have emphasized in this chapter the interlinkage of different parts of the medical care system. When we design health care policy, we cannot deal with the elderly in isolation from the rest of society. This is perhaps most true about the uninsured. Traditionally, medical payments from private and public insurers were generous. At least part of this generosity paid for care for the uninsured, which benefited us all.

As we cut back on the generosity of insurance, we should not be surprised if the market provides less of this public good. After all, the hallmark of competitive markets is that we get what we pay for. If we want to keep this flow of public good—and it seems to me that we do—we need to bring back to the table the question of how we are going to pay for it. As we move forward on some margins, it would be a shame to move backward on others.

References

Aaron, Henry. *Serious and Unstable Condition: Financing America's Health Care.* Washington, D.C.: Brookings Institution, 1991.

Chassin, Mark, et al. "Does Inappropriate Use Explain Geographic Variations in the Use of Health Care Services?" *Journal of the American Medical Association* 258 (1987): 2533–37.

Cutler, David M. "The Incidence of Adverse Medical Outcomes under Prospective Payment." *Econometrica*, February 1995, pp. 29–50.

Cutler, David M., and Mark McClellan. "The Determinants of Technological Change in Heart Attack Treatment." NBER working paper No. 5751, September 1996.

Cutler, David M., Mark McClellan, and Joseph P. Newhouse. "Productivity and Prices in Managed Care Insurance." Mimeo, Harvard University, 1997.

Cutler, David M., Mark McClellan, Joseph P. Newhouse, and Dahlia Remler. "Are Medical Prices Declining?" NBER working paper No. 5750, September 1996.

Greenspan, Allan M., et al. "Incidence of Unwarranted Implantation of Permanent Cardiac Pacemakers in a Large Medical Population." *New England Journal of Medicine* 318 (1988): 158–63.

Kahn, Katherine L., et al. "Comparing Outcomes of Care before and after Implementation of the DRG-Based Prospective Payment System." *Journal of the American Medical Association* 264 (1990).

Manning, Willard, et al. "Health Insurance and the Demand for Medical Care: Evidence from a Randomized Experiment." *American Economic Review*, 1987.

McClellan, Mark, and Joseph P. Newhouse. "The Marginal Benefits of Medical Progress." Mimeo, Harvard University, 1995.

Newhouse, Joseph P. "Medical Care Costs: How Much Welfare Loss?" *Journal of Economic Perspectives*, 1992.

———. *Free for All? Lessons from the Rand Health Insurance Experiment.* Cambridge, Mass.: Harvard University Press, 1993.

Staiger, Doug, and Gary Gaumer. "The Effect of Prospective Payment on Post-Hospital Mortality." Mimeo, Harvard University, 1990.

Weisbrod, Burt. "The Health Care Quadrilemma: An Essay on Technological Change, Insurance, Quality of Care, and Cost Containment." *Journal of Economic Literature*, June 1991, pp. 523–52.

Wennberg, Jack E., J. L. Freeman, and W. J. Culp. "Are Hospital Services

Rationed in New Haven or Over-Utilized in Boston?" *Lancet* 1 (May 23, 1987): 1185–88.

Winslow, Constance M., et al. "The Appropriateness of Carotid Endarterectomy." *New England Journal of Medicine* 318 (1988a): 721–27.

———. "The Appropriateness of Performing Coronary Artery Bypass Surgery." *Journal of the American Medical Association* 260 (1988b): 505–10.

Contributors

B. DOUGLAS BERNHEIM is the Lewis and Virginia Eaton Professor of Economics at Stanford University. He received an A.B. in economics from Harvard University and a Ph.D. in economics from MIT in 1982. His previous academic positions include endowed chairs in the Department of Finance at Northwestern University's J. L. Kellogg Graduate School of Management and in the Department of Economics at Princeton University, where he also served as the codirector of the Center for Economic Policy Studies. He is a research associate of the National Bureau of Economic Research and a fellow of the Econometric Society.

DAVID M. CUTLER is the John L. Loeb Associate Professor of Social Sciences at Harvard University. He received a B.A., summa cum laude, from Harvard College and a Ph.D. in economics from MIT. He is also a faculty research fellow in the Public Economics and Aging and Health Care Programs at the National Bureau of Economic Research.

JOHN B. SHOVEN is the Charles R. Schwab Professor of Economics and dean of the School of Humanities and Sciences, Stanford University, and a research associate of the National Bureau of Economic Research.

DAVID A. WISE is the John F. Stambaugh Professor of Political Economy at the John F. Kennedy School of Government, Harvard University; the area director of Health and Retirement Programs at the National Bureau of Economic Research; and a senior fellow at the Hoover Institution.

Index